César
FRANCK

VARIATIONS SYMPHONIQUES
pour Piano et Orchestre
FWV 46
(1885)

Study Score
Partitur

PETRUCCI LIBRARY PRESS

ORCHESTRA

2 Flutes

2 Oboes

2 Clarinets

2 Bassoons

4 Horns

2 Trumpets

Timpani

Violins I

Violins II

Violas

Cellos

Double Basses

Duration: ca. 15 minutes

First performance:
Paris: May 1, 1886
Louis Diémer, piano solo
Orchestre de Société Nationale de Musique
César Franck, conductor

ISBN: 978-1-60874-124-3
This score is a slightly modified unabridged reprint of the score
issued in 1893 by Enoch, Frères et Costallat, Paris, plate E. F. & C. 2164.
The score has been scaled to fit the present format.

Printed in the USA
First Printing: September, 2015

Variations Symphoniques

FWV 46

César Franck (1822-1890)

Petrucci Library Press

Più lento.
ad lib.
Poco all°
Piano.
mf espress
dim.
ff
Vons
Altos.
p
Vellles et C.B.
Più lento.
Poco all°
Più lento.
ad lib.
mf espress.
dim.
p
Più lento.
Poco rall.
A
Poco all°
dim.
p
Poco rall.
Poco all°

19
Clar.
Bns
1o
1er et 2e Cors.
pp
19
Piano.
Vons
sf
Altos.
Vcelles
23
1o
23

27
Clar.
B^ns
1er et 2e Cors.
à 2
mf cresc.
27
Piano.
espress.
cresc.
V^ns
cresc.
Altos.
Div.
V^lles et C. B.
31 Fl.
à 2
f
ff
molto
dim.
Hautb.
Clar.
1er et 2e Cors.
31
Piano.
V^ns
Altos.
V^lles et C. B.

B
34 Fl.
L'istesso Tempo.
pp
Hautb.
pp
Clar.
à 2
pp
Bns
Cors.
pp
pp
Tromp.
1º
pp
Timb.
p
34
pp
Piano.
pp
pp
L'istesso Tempo.
pizz.
mf
pp
Vns
Div.
pizz.
mf
pp
Altos.
Div.
pizz.
mf
pp
Velles
Div.
pizz.
mf
pp
C. B.
pizz.
mf
pp
L'istesso Tempo.

40
pp
pp
à 2
pp
pp
pp
pp
pp
pp
40
8
pp
arco.
pizz.
p
arco.
pizz.
p
Unis.
arco.
pizz.
p
arco.
pizz.
p
pp
arco.
Unis.
arco.
arco.
pizz.
p
arco.
pp

46
Poco rall.
C
Poco più lento.
pp
pp
46
Poco rall.
Poco più lento.
Poco rall.
Poco più lento.

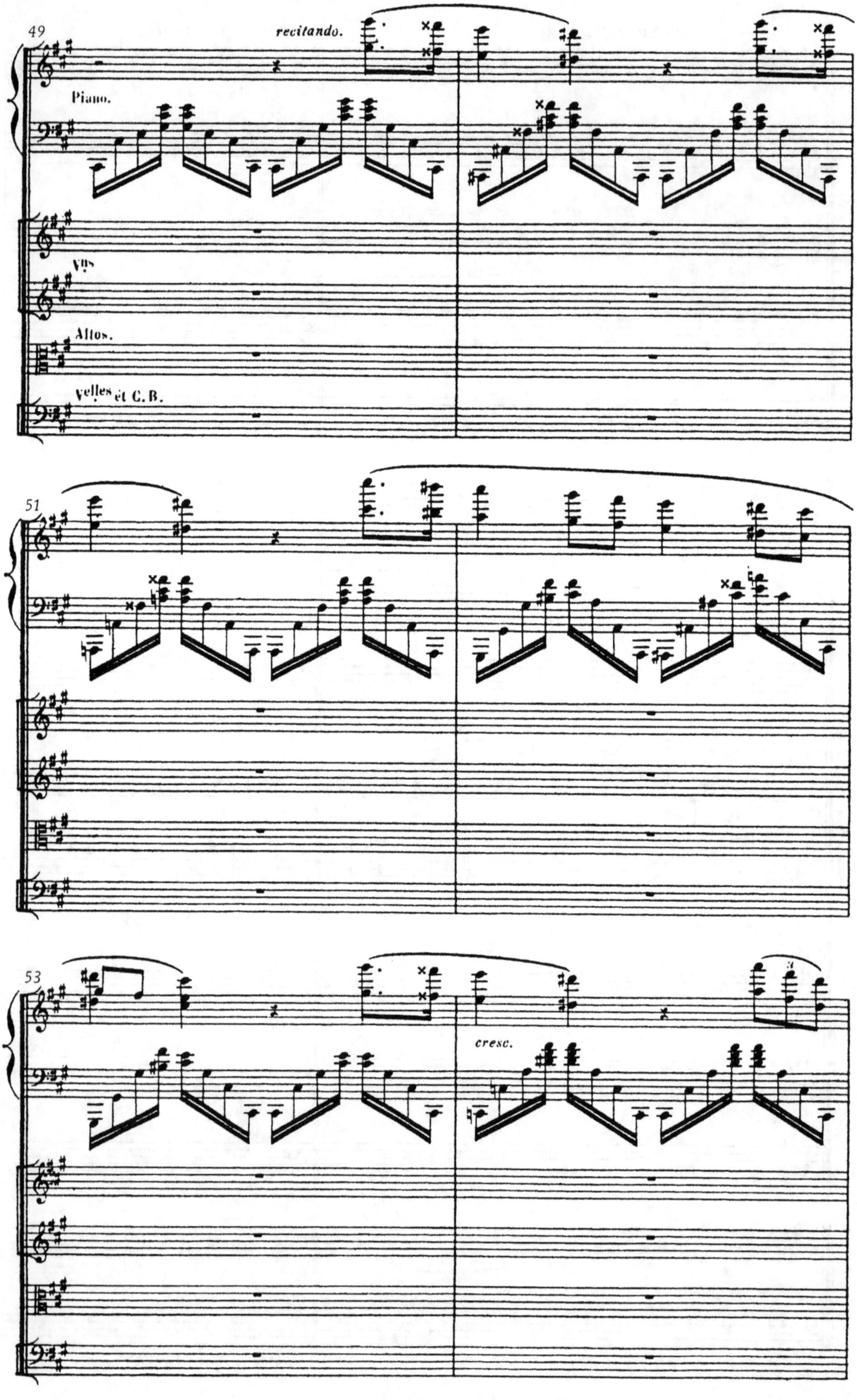
49
recitando.
Piano.
Vns
Altos.
velles et C.B.
51
53
cresc.

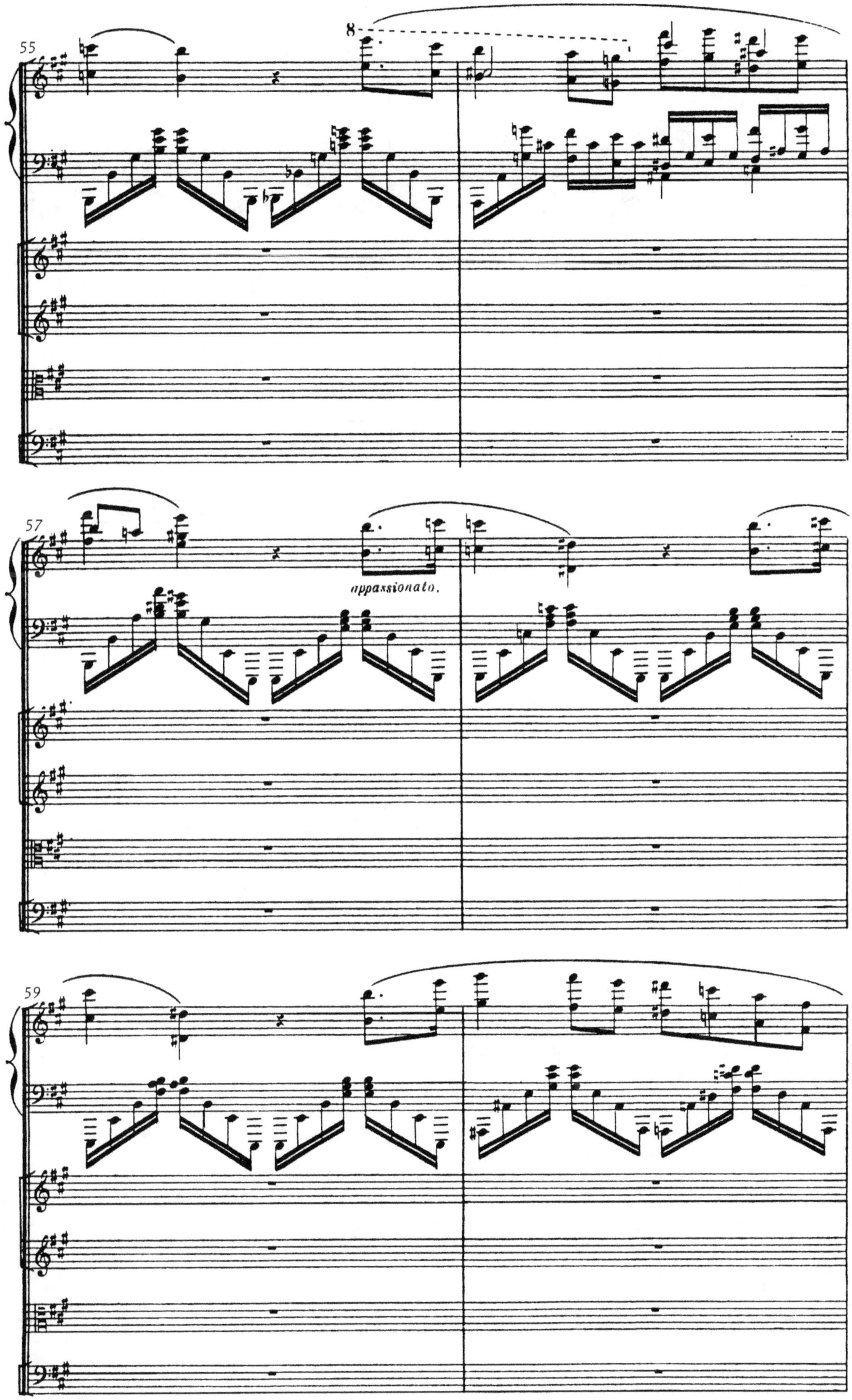
55
8
57
appassionato.
59

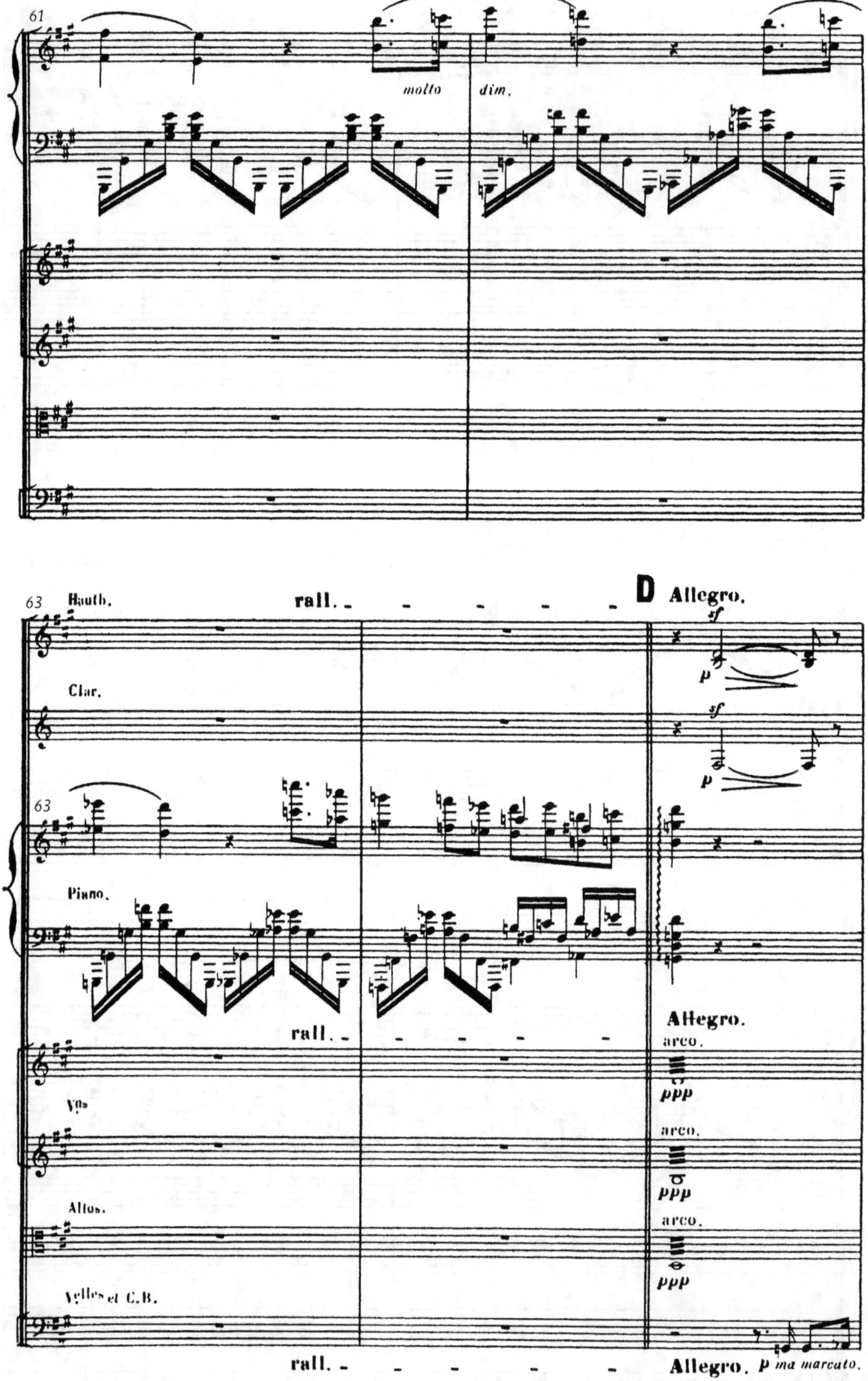
61
molto
dim.
63
Hautb.
rall.
D
Allegro.
sf
p
Clar.
sf
p
63
Piano.
rall.
Allegro.
arco.
ppp
Vons
arco.
ppp
Altos.
arco.
ppp
Vlles et C.B.
rall.
Allegro.
p ma marcato.

66
Fl.
Hauth.
Clar.
à 2.
Bns
1º
Cors.
Tromp.
Piano.
Vns
Altos.
Velles et C.B.
più marcato.

Animato.
71
Fl.
Hauth.
à 2.
Clar.
à 2.
Bns
à 2.
Cors.
à 2.
Tromp.
8
71
Piano.
cresc
Animato.
Vns
Altos.
Vlles et C.B.
Animato.

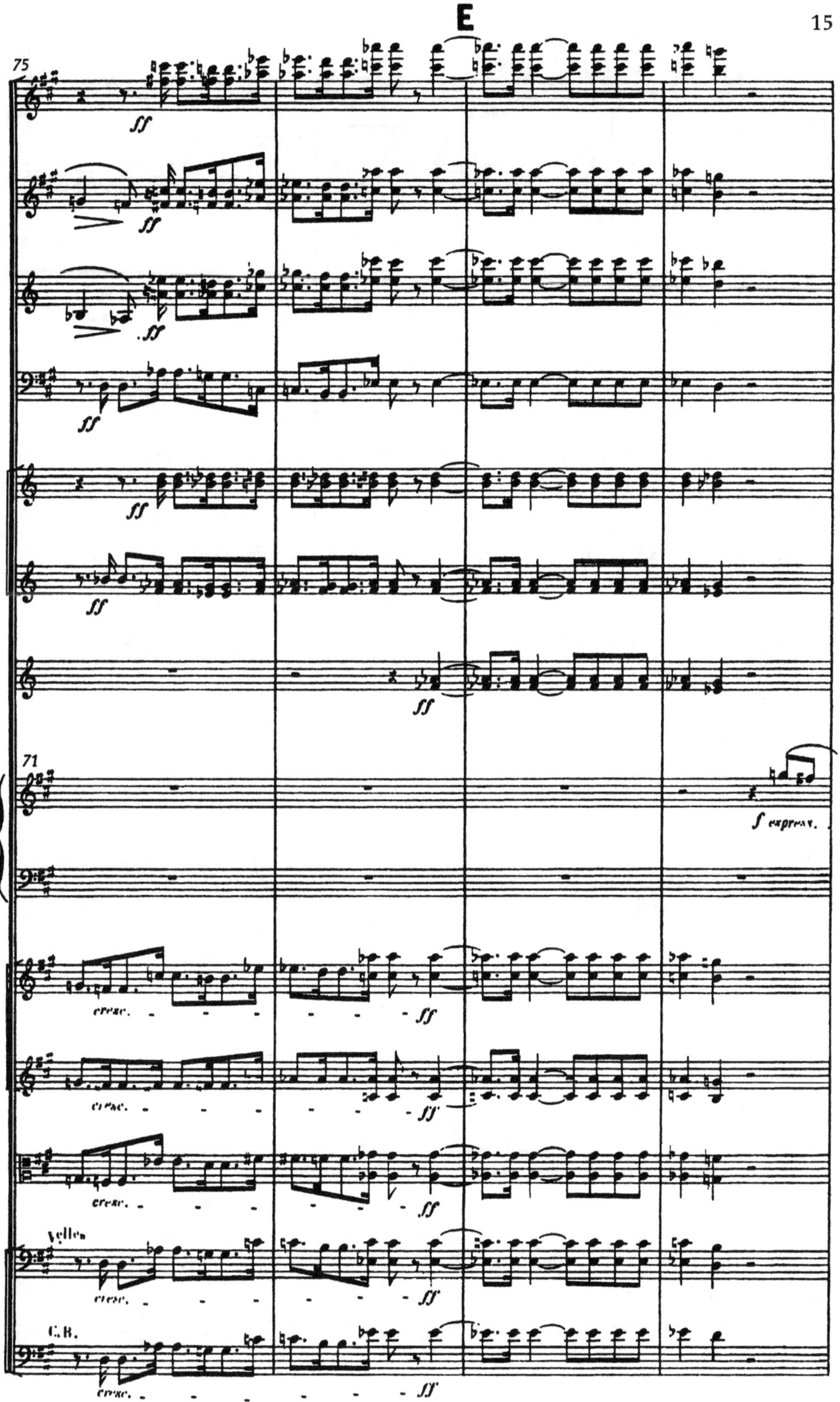
E
75
ff
71
f express.
cresc.
Celles
C.B.

79
Piano.
dolce.
sempre dim.
Vlns sempre ff
mf
p
sempre ff
Altos.
Velles
C.B.
poco a poco rall.
84
molto teneramente con fantasia.
poco a poco rall.
pp
poco a poco rall.

90
Fl.
Hautb.
Clar.
Bns
Cors.
Timb.
Piano.
Vns
Altos.
Velles
C.B.
Allto quasi Andte
Allto quasi Andte
Allto quasi Andte
ppp
p
pp
pizz.
Div.
mf
mf espress.

94
Poco rall.
a Tempo.
meno p
1º
mf
94
mf
espress. con simplicita.
Poco rall.
a Tempo.
arco.
pp
Unis. arco.
pp
arco.
pp
arco.
dim.
f
dim.
pp
Poco rall.
a Tempo.

101
Piano.
più f
Vns
Altos.
Vclles et C. B.
108
dolce.
più f
dim
F
114
dolce
espress.
dolce
Div
p
Unis
p
Vclles
p
C. B.
p

120
Div.
Unis
125
Fl.
p
Hauth
Clar.
p
p
p
125
Piano.
molto rinf.
f molto sost.
Div.
Unis
Altos.
f
Velles et C.B.
f

G
131
Fl.
1º
pp
Hauth.
1º
pp
Clar.
pp
pp
Bns
1º
pp
2º pp
1er et 2e Cors.
1º
pp
131
Piano.
dolce.
sempre dolce.
Vns
dim.
p
dim.
p
Altos.
dim.
p
dolce molto cantabile.
Velles
dim
p
dolce molto cantabile.
C.B.
dim
p
Div.
pp

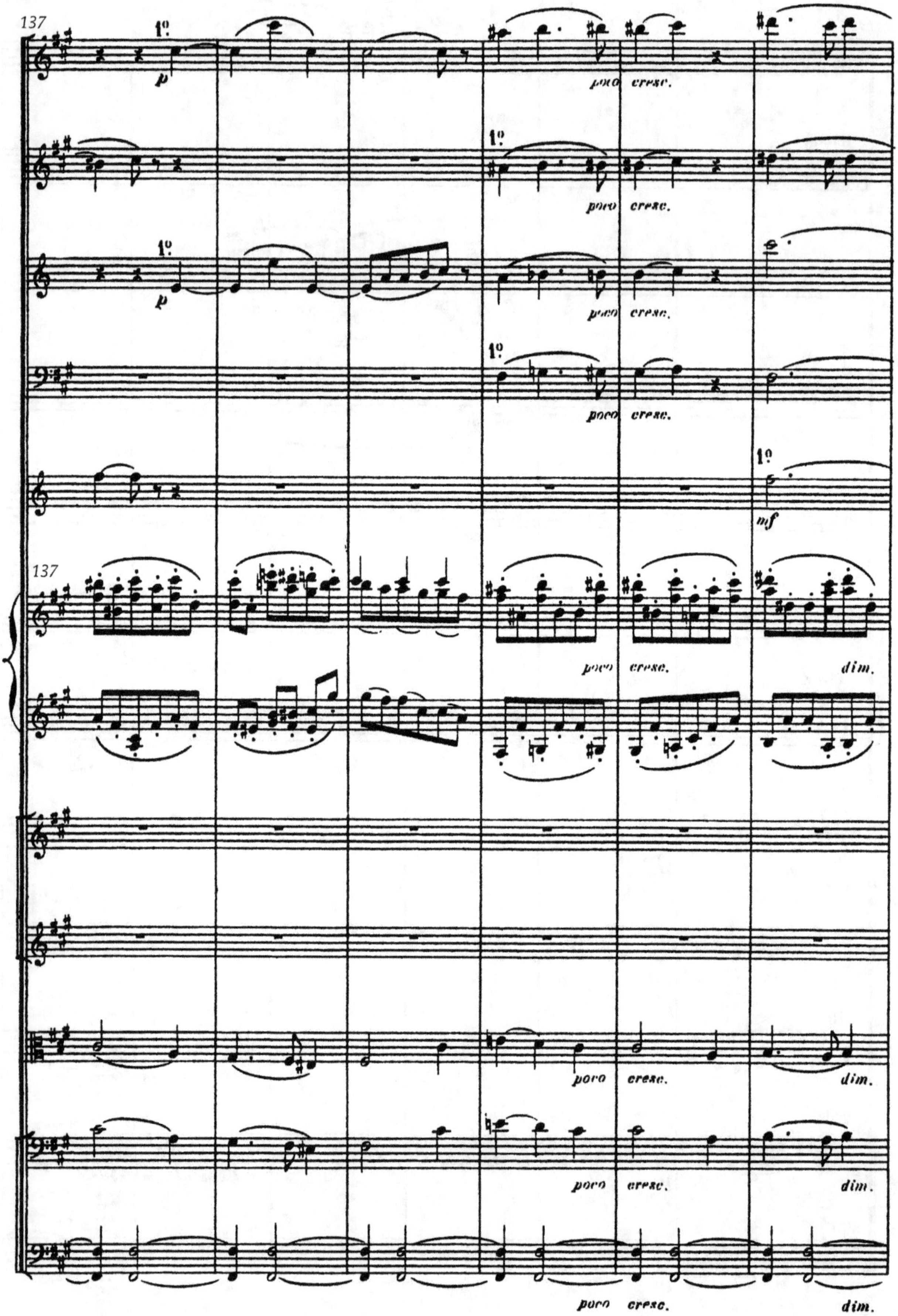
137
1º
p
poco cresc.
mf
dim.

143
dim.
dim.
1º
dim.
dim.
1º
dim.
143
dolce cantabile.
pp
pp
dolce molto cantabile.
pp
dolce molto cantabile.
pp

rall.
H
a Tempo.
149
pp
dim.
pp
dim.
1º
dim.
149
pp
dim.
mf legato.
rall.
a Tempo.
dim.
dim.
dim.
rall.
a Tempo.

154
Piano
pizz.
mf
Vns.
pizz.
mf
Altos.
pizz.
mf
Vcelles
pizz.
mf
C. B.
157
f
f
f
f
Unis pizz.
f

160
1º
p espress.
Hautb.
1º
p espress.
Ier et 2e Cors.
à 2
p
154
Piano.
p
Vns
p
p
p
p
163
cresc.
cresc.
cresc.
à 2
163
8
cresc.
molto cresc.
cresc.
cresc.
cresc.
cresc.
cresc.
cresc.
cresc.
cresc.
Div.
cresc.

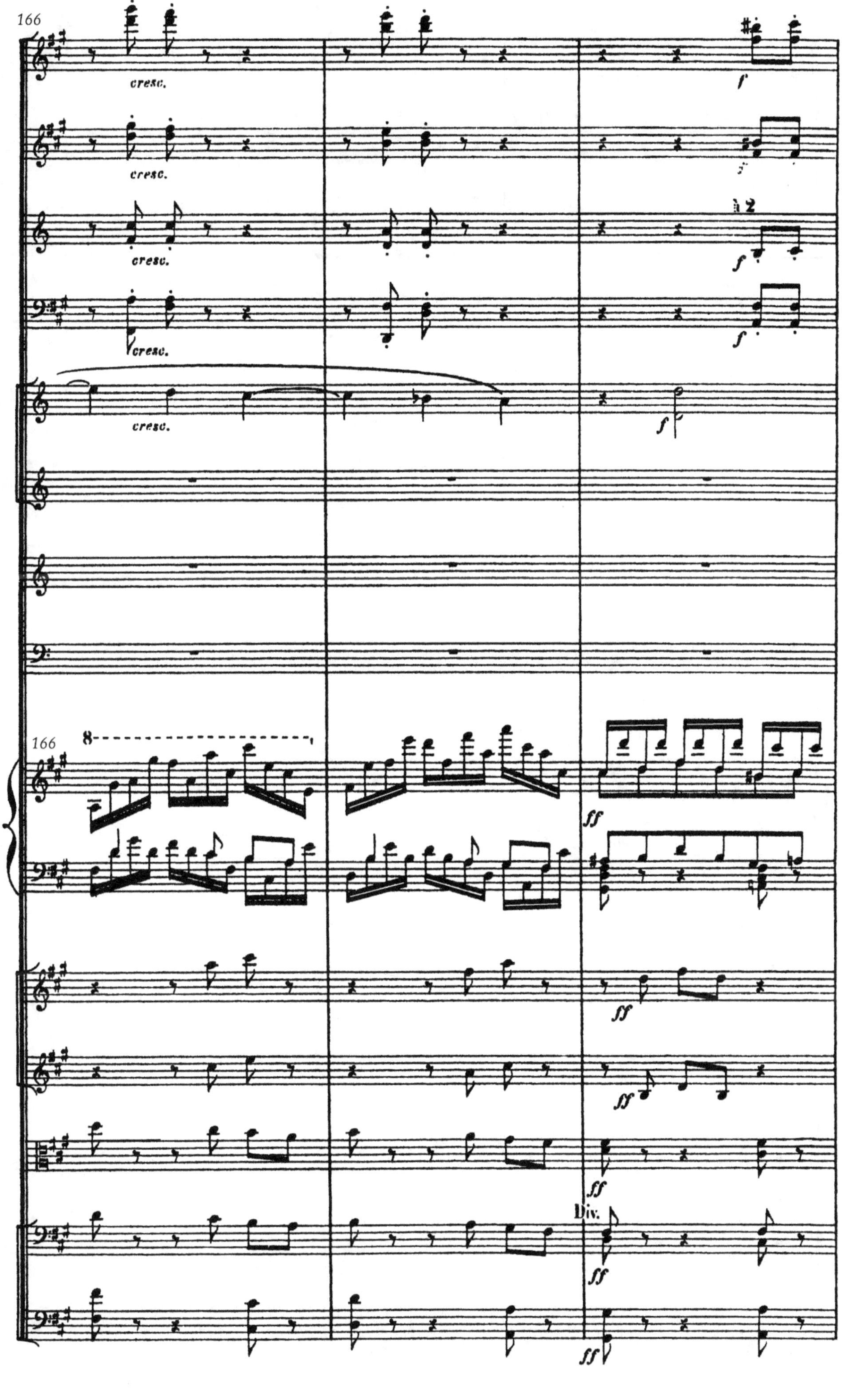
166
cresc.
f
Div.
ff
8

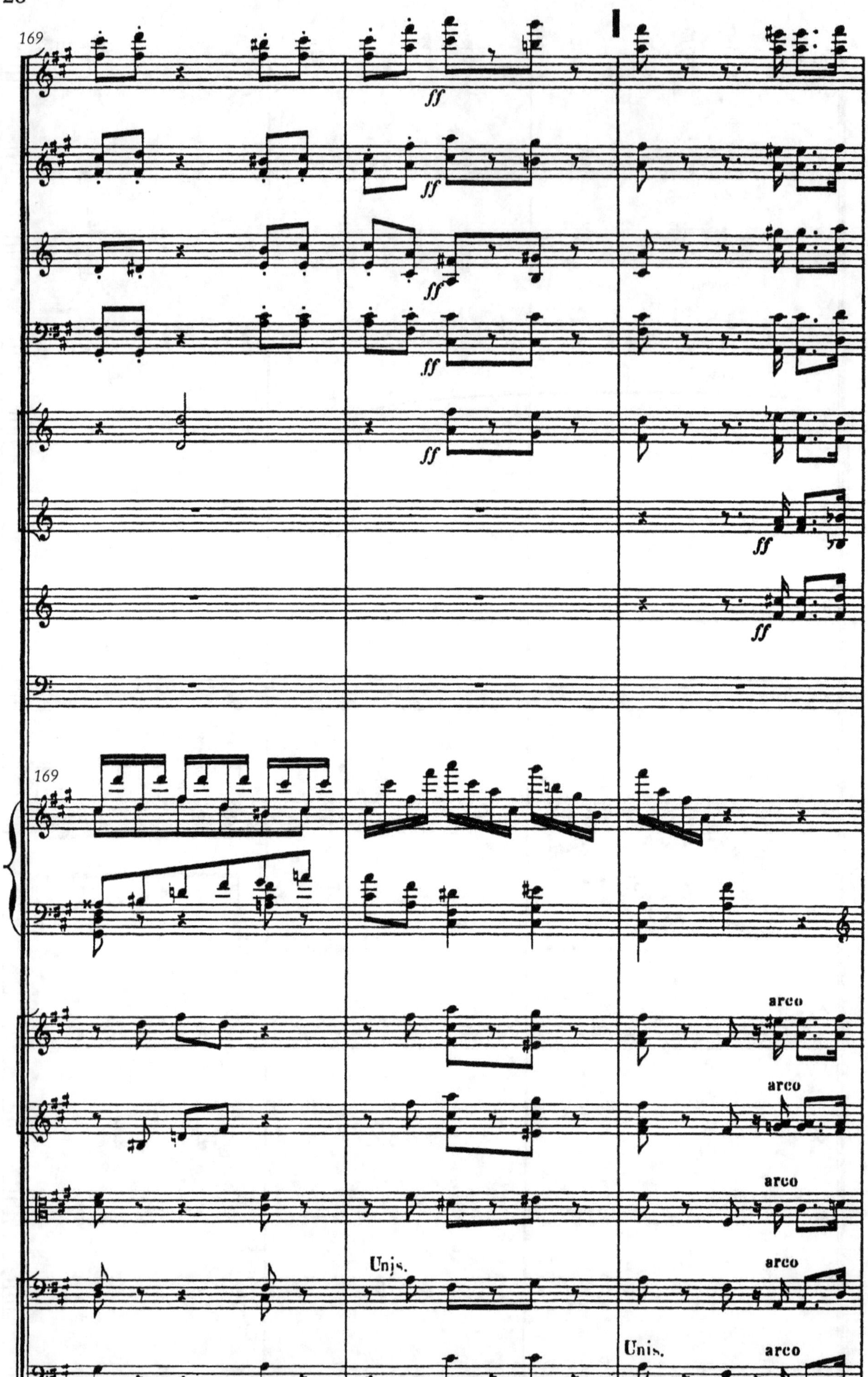
169
I
ff
ff
ff
ff
ff
ff
ff
169
arco
arco
arco
Unjs.
arco
Unis.
arco

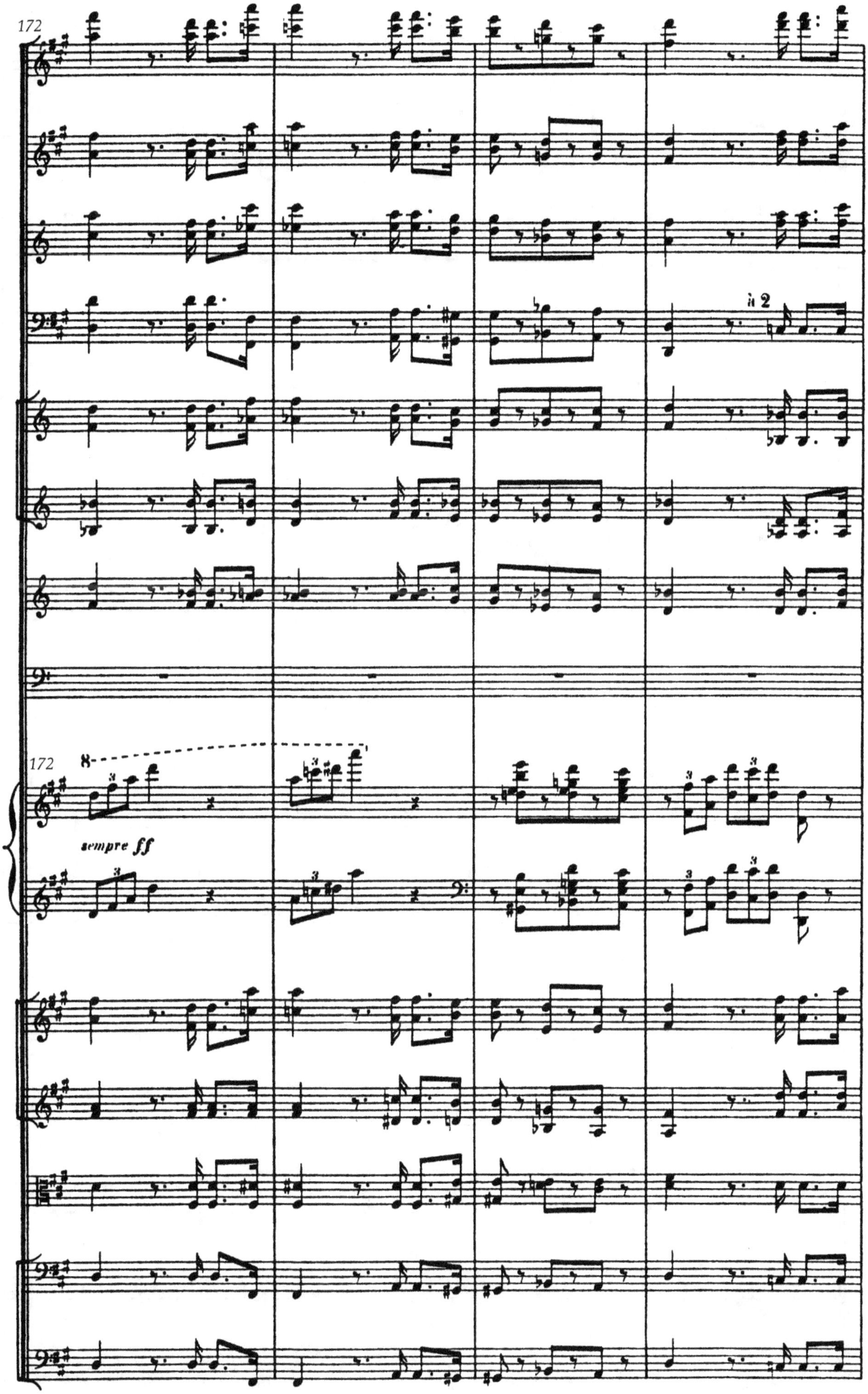
172
à 2
172
8
sempre ff

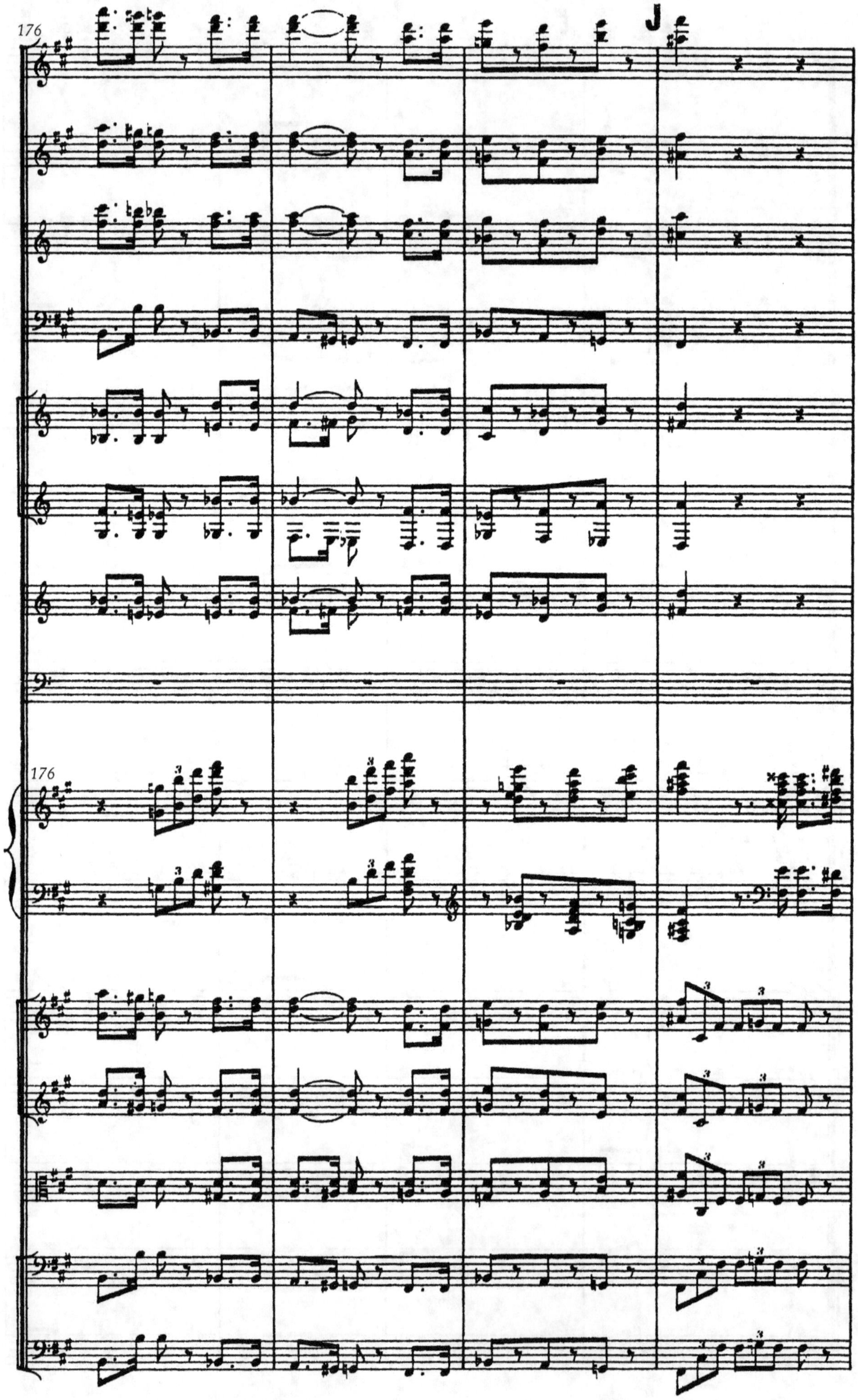
176
J
176

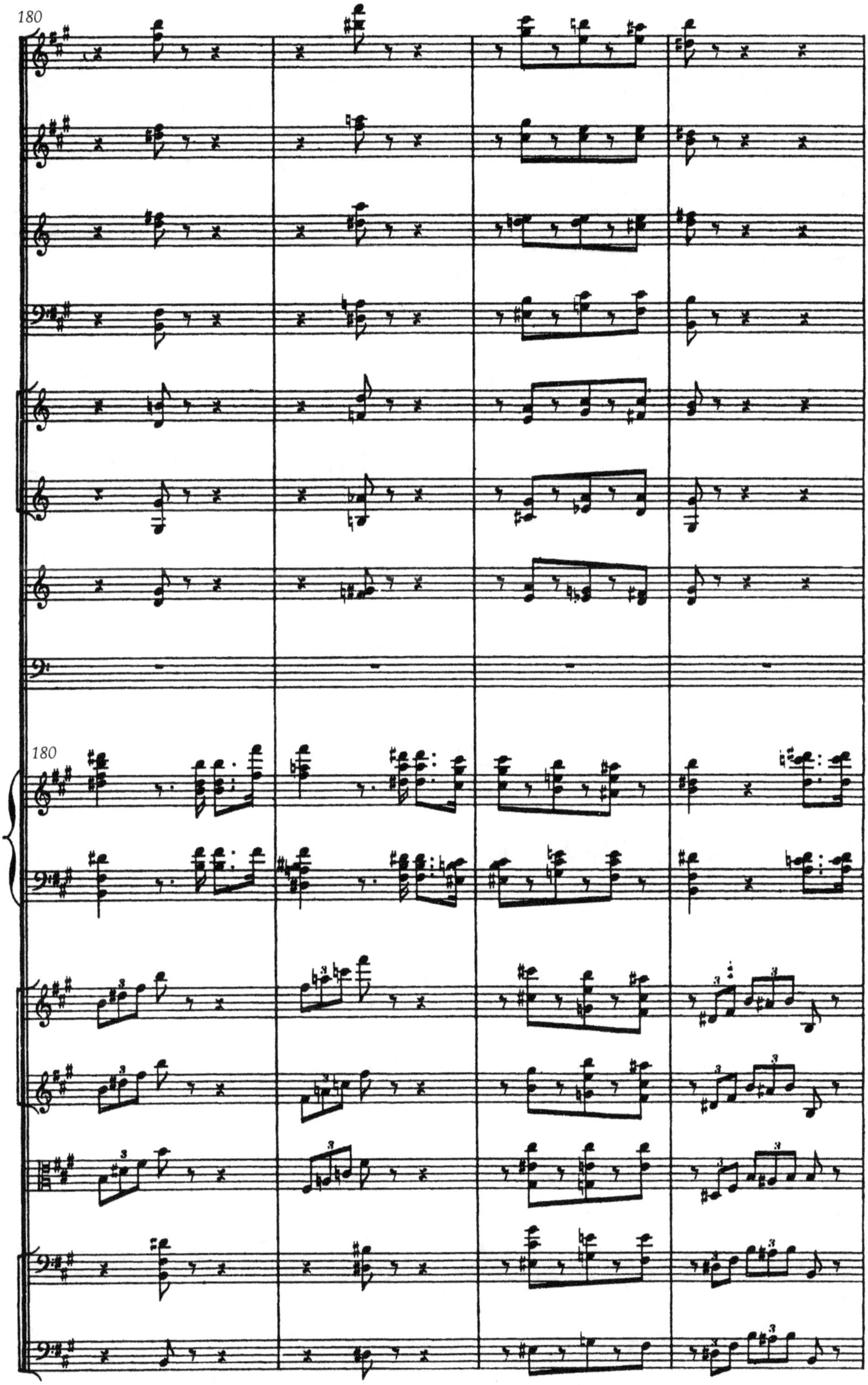
180
180

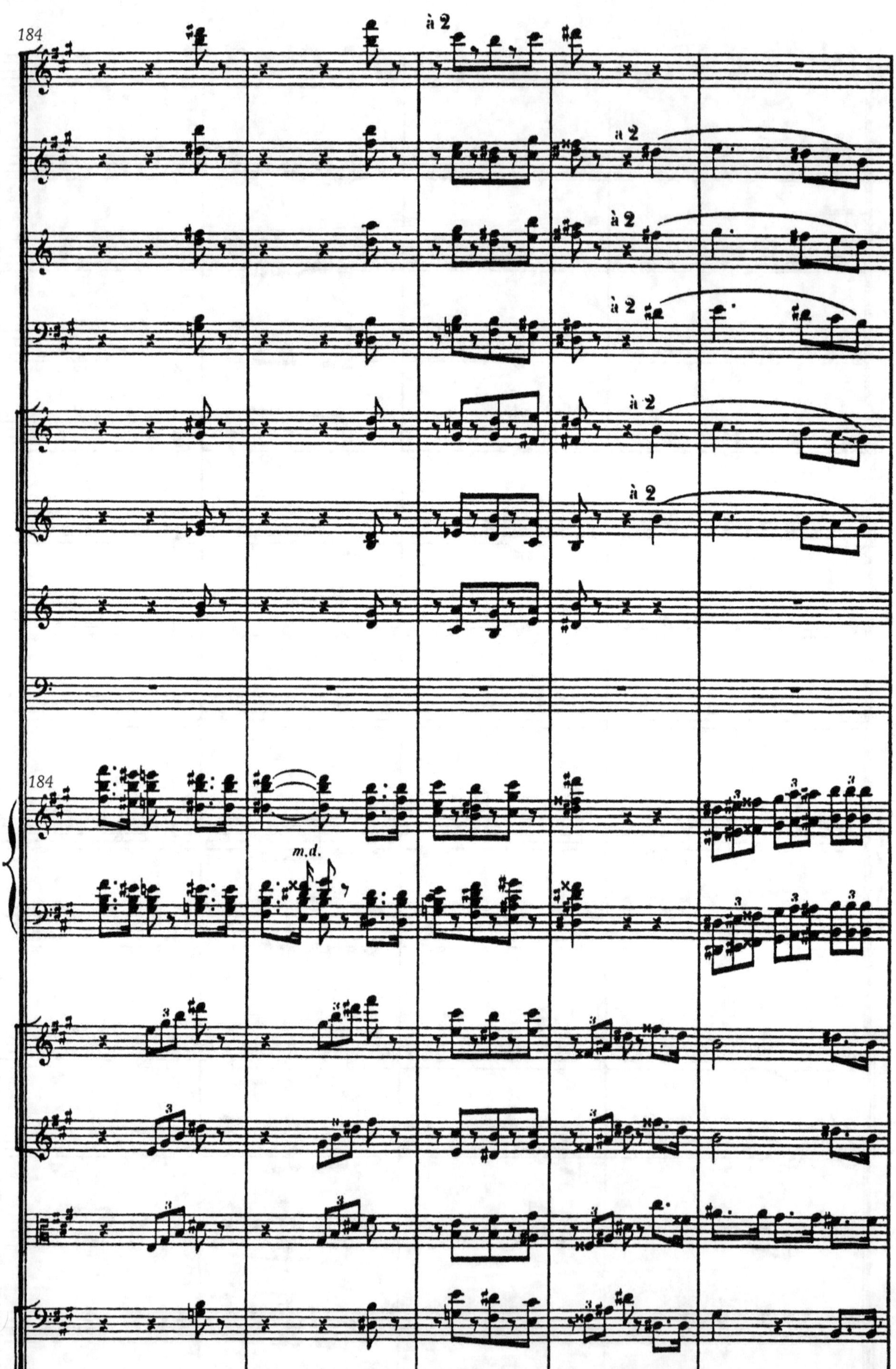
184
à 2
à 2
à 2
à 2
à 2
à 2
184
m.d.
3

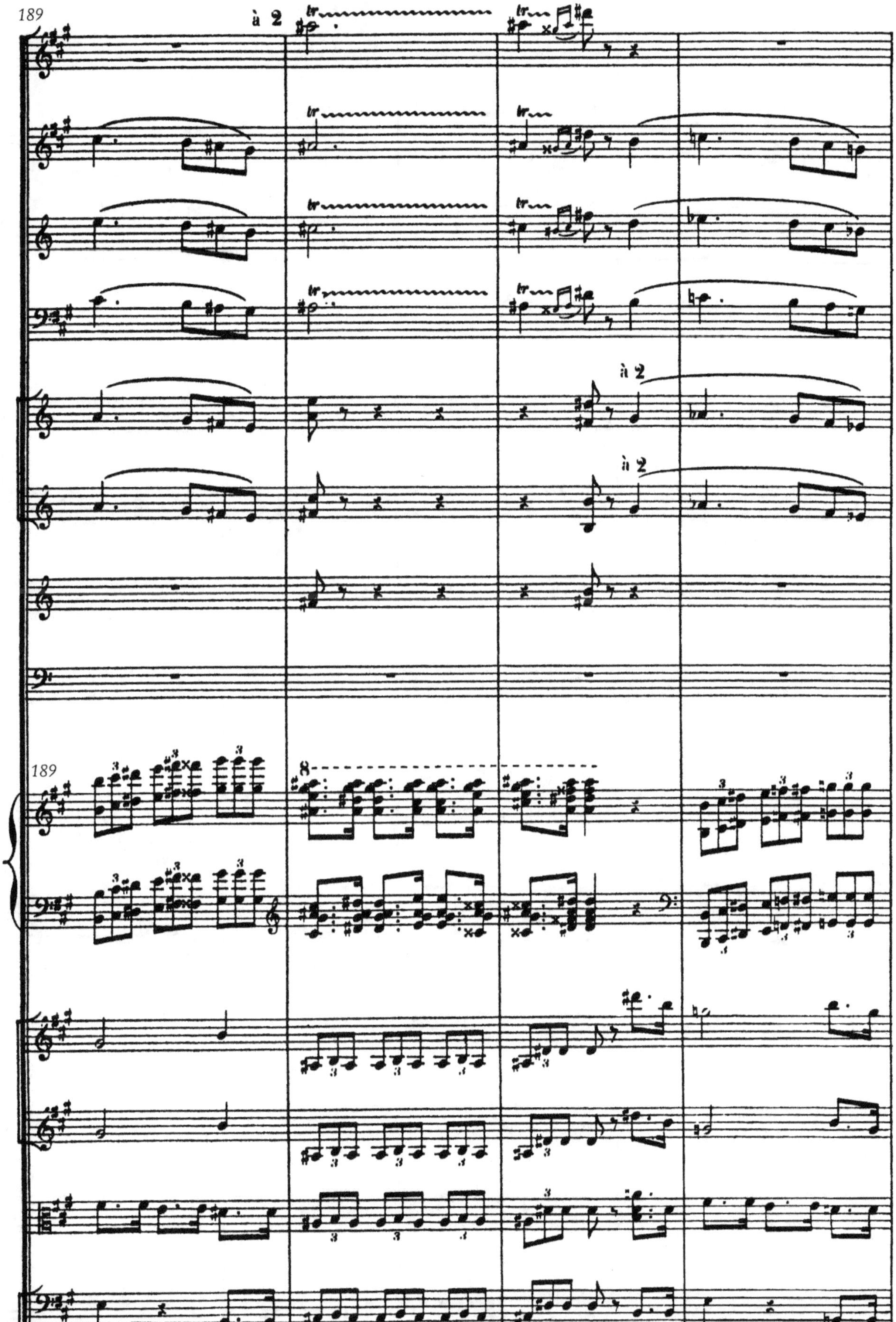
189
à 2
tr
à 2
à 2
189
8

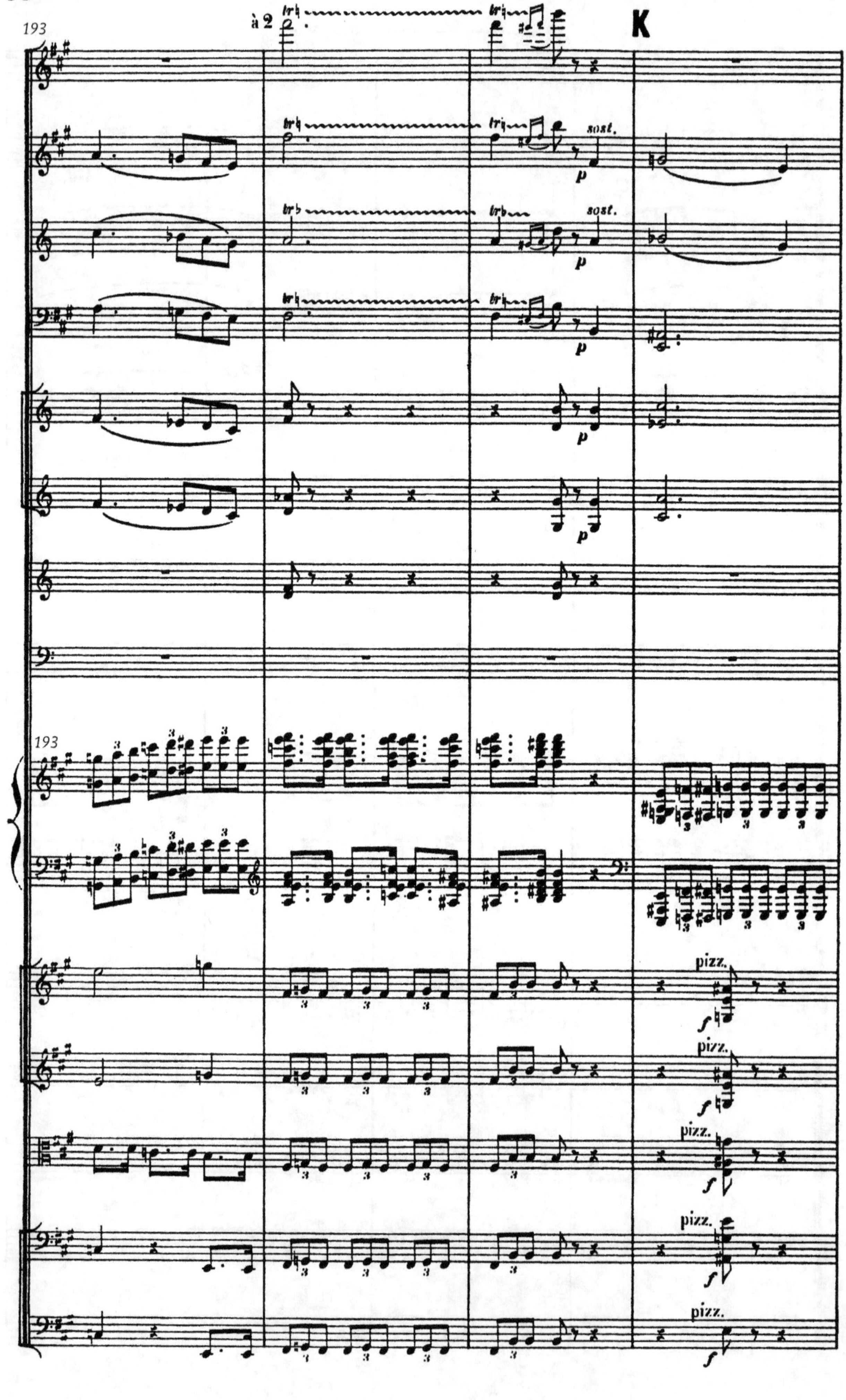
193
à 2
K
sost.
sost.
193
pizz.
pizz.
pizz.
pizz.
pizz.

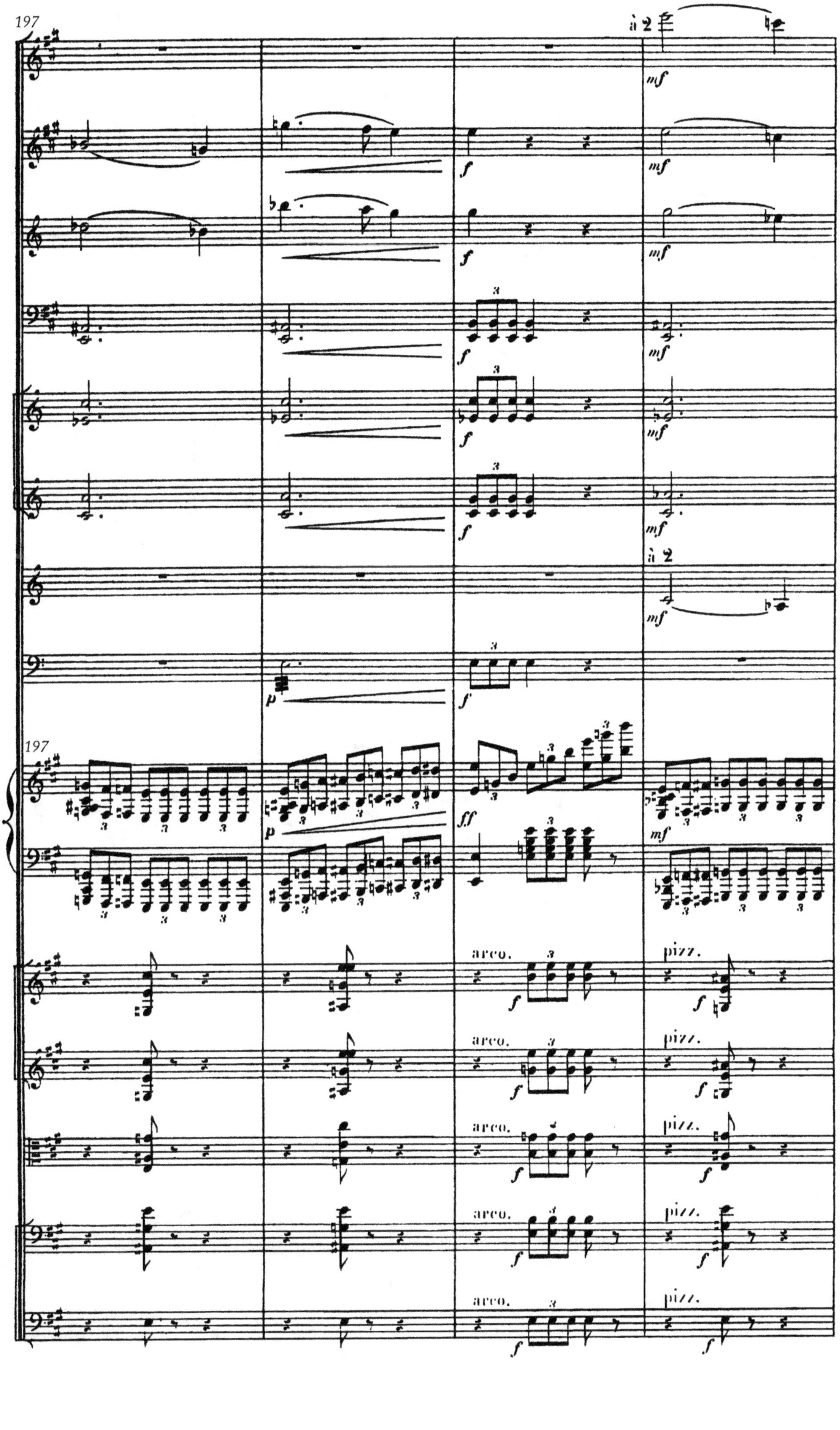
197
à 2
mf
f
p
ff
arco.
pizz.

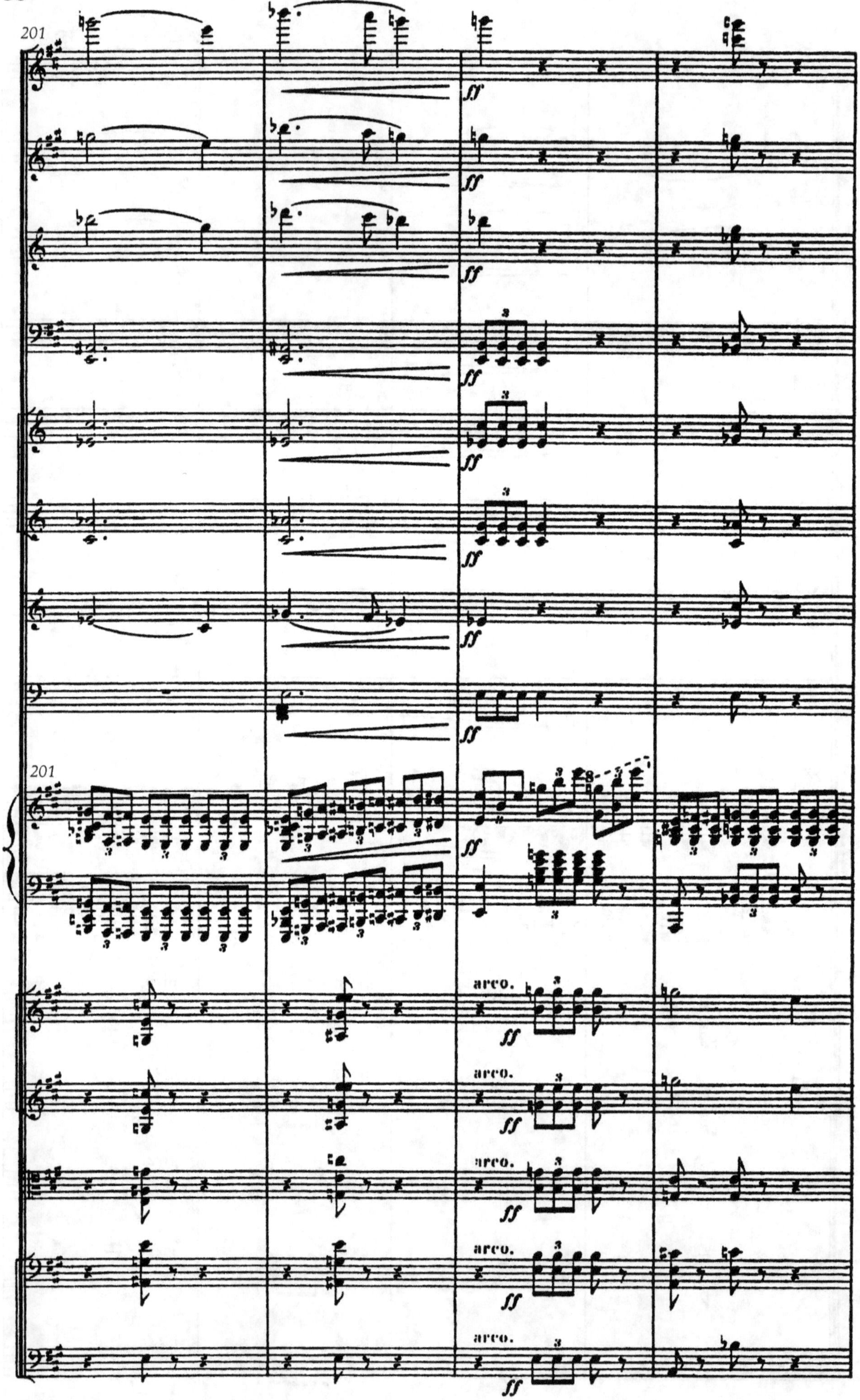
201
201
arco.
arco.
arco.
arco.
arco.

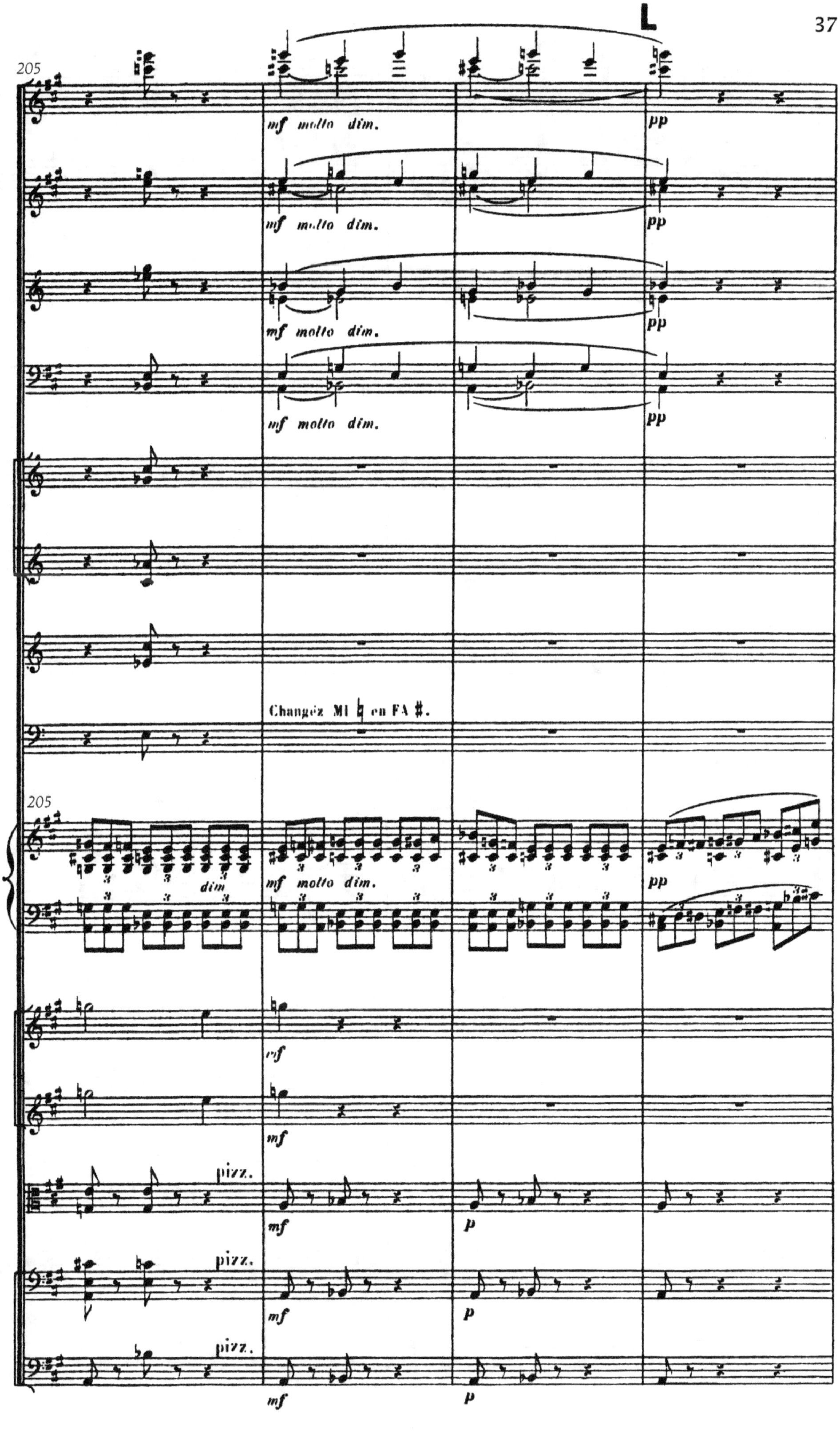
L
205
mf molto dim.
pp
Changéz MI ♮ en FA ♯.
dim
pizz.
mf
p

209
Piano.
pp
Vlns
pp
Altos.
arco.
pp
Vcelles
arco.
Div. pp
C. B.
arco.
pp
213
Piano.
Vlns
Altos.
Vcelles
C. B.

217
Fl.
Clar.
Bns
Piano.
Vns
Altos.
expres.
Vlles et C.B.
221
Fl.
Clar.
Bns.
1er et 2e Cors.
Piano.
Vns
Altos.
Vlles
Div.
C.B.

225
Hauth.
molto rall.
1°
pp
Clar.
1°
2°
pp
Bns
pp
1r et 2e Cors.
pp
225
Piano.
molto rall.
Vns
Unis.
sost.
p dolce.
230
M
Molto più lento.
Clar.
Bns
Cors.
230
Piano.
pp express.
sempre legatissimo.
Molto più lento.
Vns

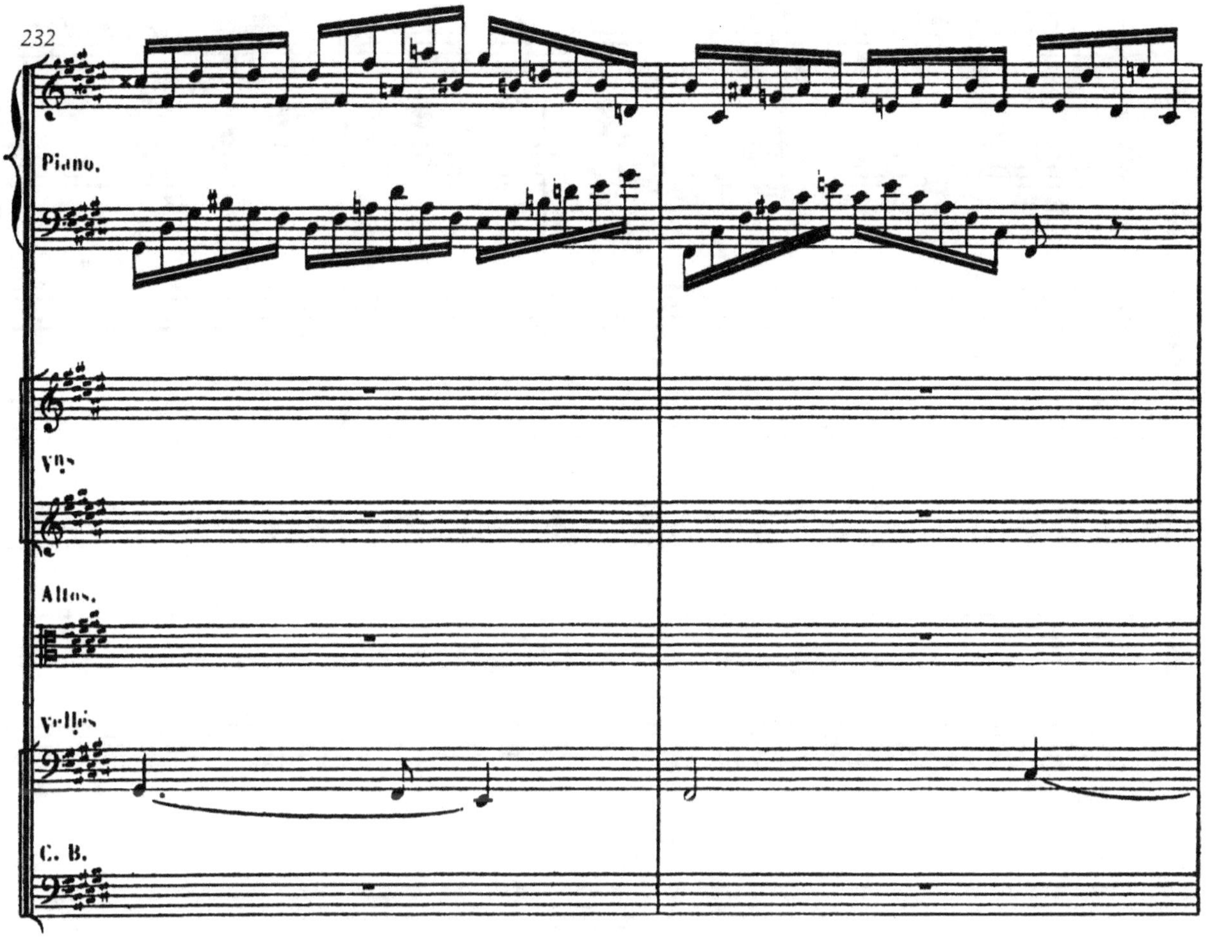
232
Piano.
Vns
Altos.
Vclles
C. B.

234
Piano.
poco cresc.
Vns
Altos.
Vclles
poco cresc.
C. B.

236
Piano.
dim.
pp
pizz.
p
Vlns
Altos.
Velles
C. B.
238
Clar.
Bns
1º
Cors 1º et 2º
238
Piano.
Vlns

240
Fl.
meno dolce.
Clar.
meno dolce.
Bns
1er et 2e Cors.
1o
240
Piano.
poco cresc.
Vns
Altos.
Vlles
espress.
arco.
meno dolce.
C. B.
meno dolce.
242
Fl.
Clar.
242
Piano.
Vns
dim.

244
Clar.
Poco rall.
pp
Bns
pp
244
pp
Piano.
Poco rall.
Vns
pp
Poco rall.
246
Fl.
pp
pp
a Tempo.
Clar.
pp
246
Piano.
a Tempo.
Mettez la sourdine.
Vns
Mettez la sourdine.
Mettez la sourdine.
Mettez la sourdine.
a Tempo.

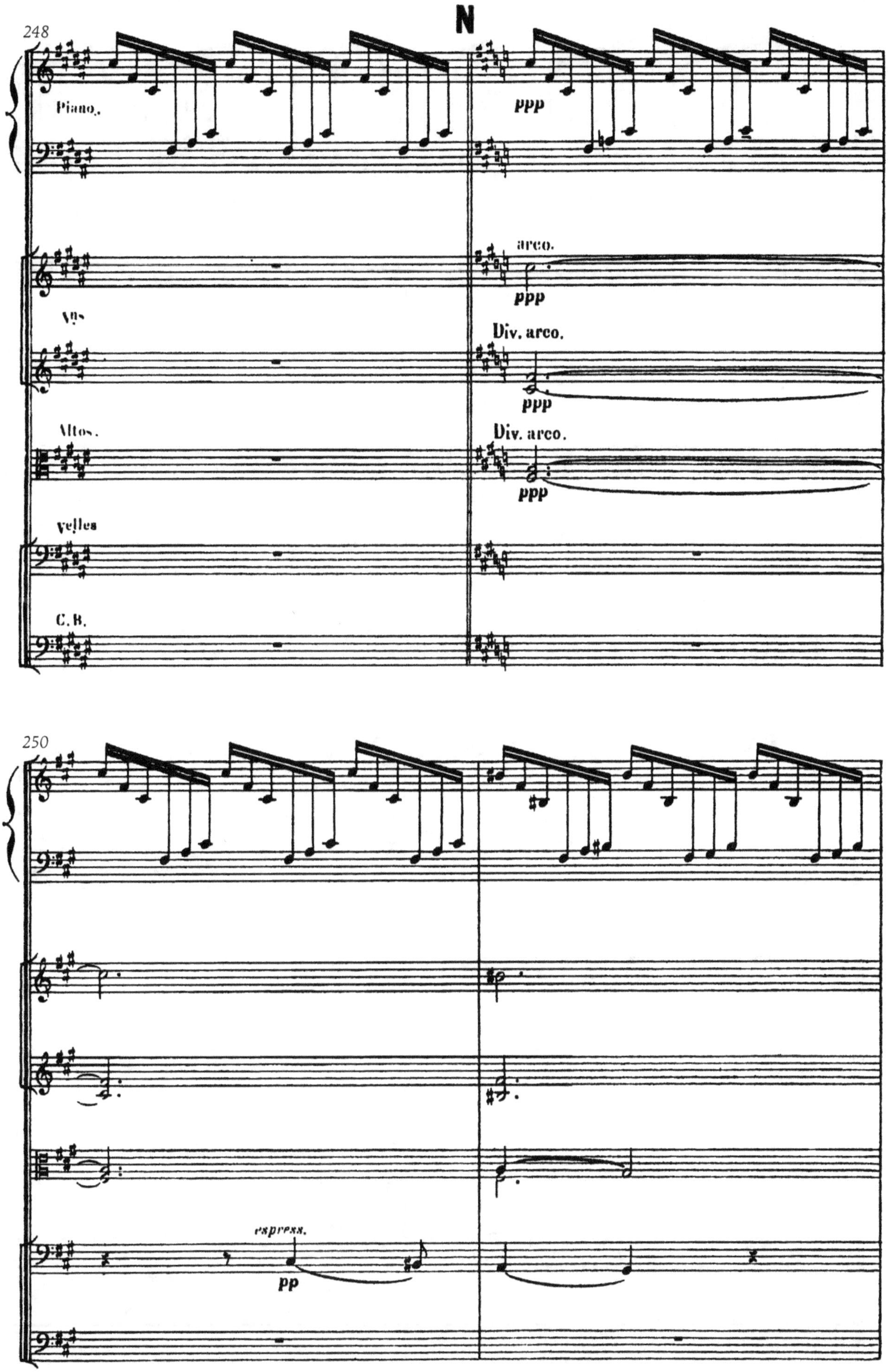
N
248
Piano.
ppp
arco.
ppp
Vns
Div. arco.
ppp
Altos.
Div. arco.
ppp
Velles
C.B.
250
espress.
pp

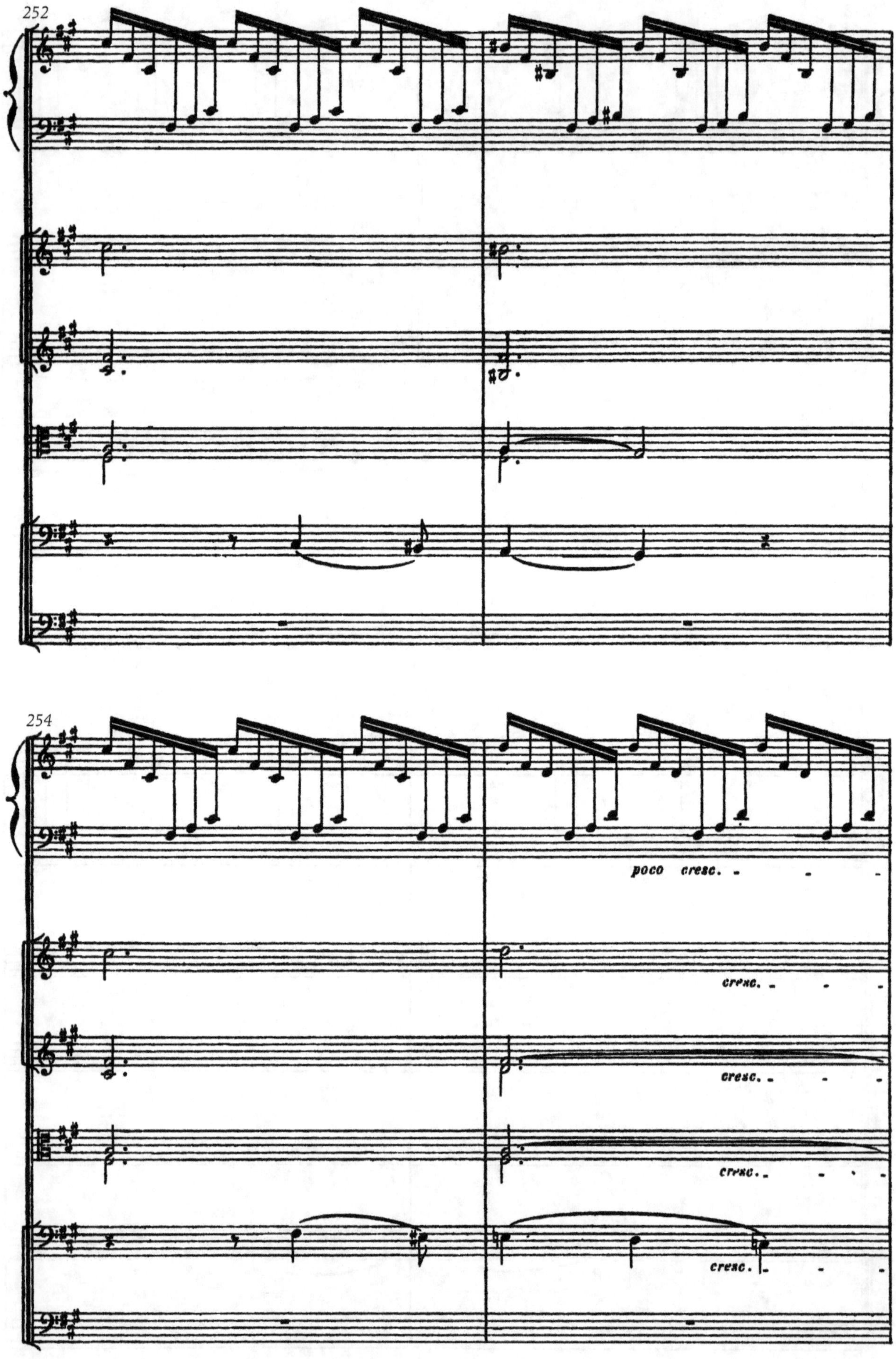
252
254
poco cresc.
cresc.
cresc.
cresc.
cresc.

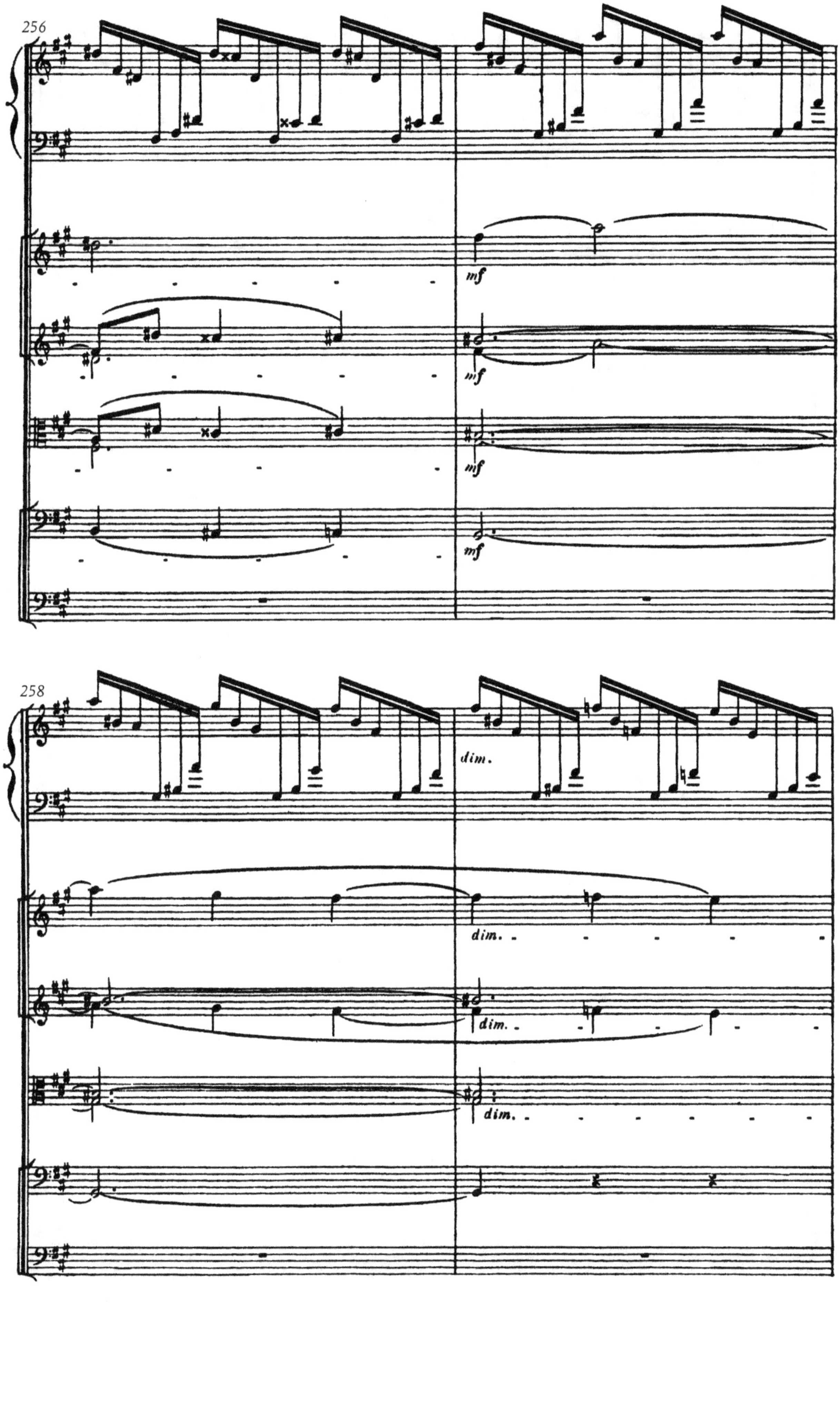
256
mf
mf
mf
mf
258
dim.
dim.
dim.
dim.

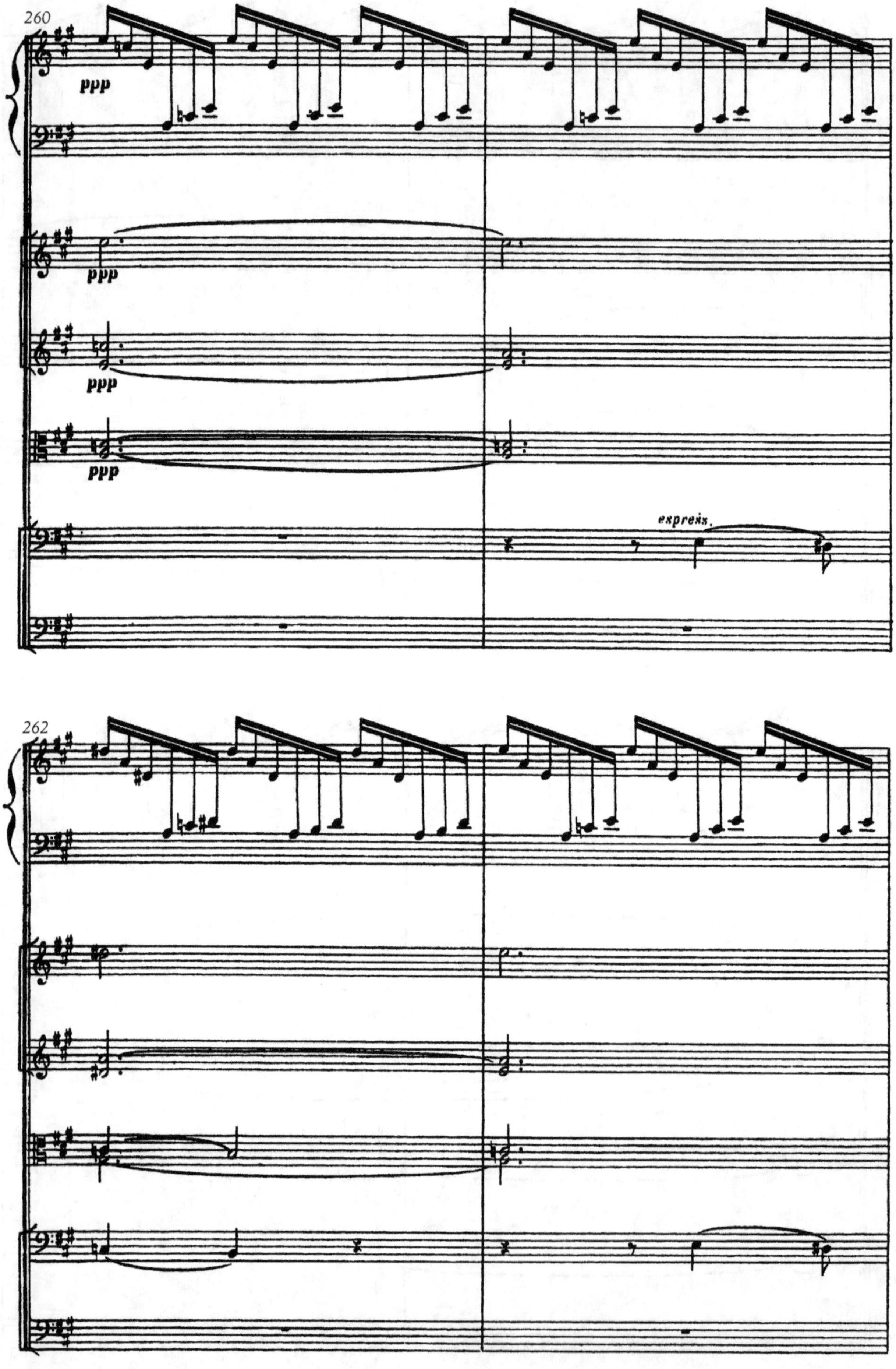
260
ppp
ppp
ppp
ppp
express.
262

264
molto
molto
molto
molto
molto

266
cresc.
cresc.
cresc.
cresc.
cresc.

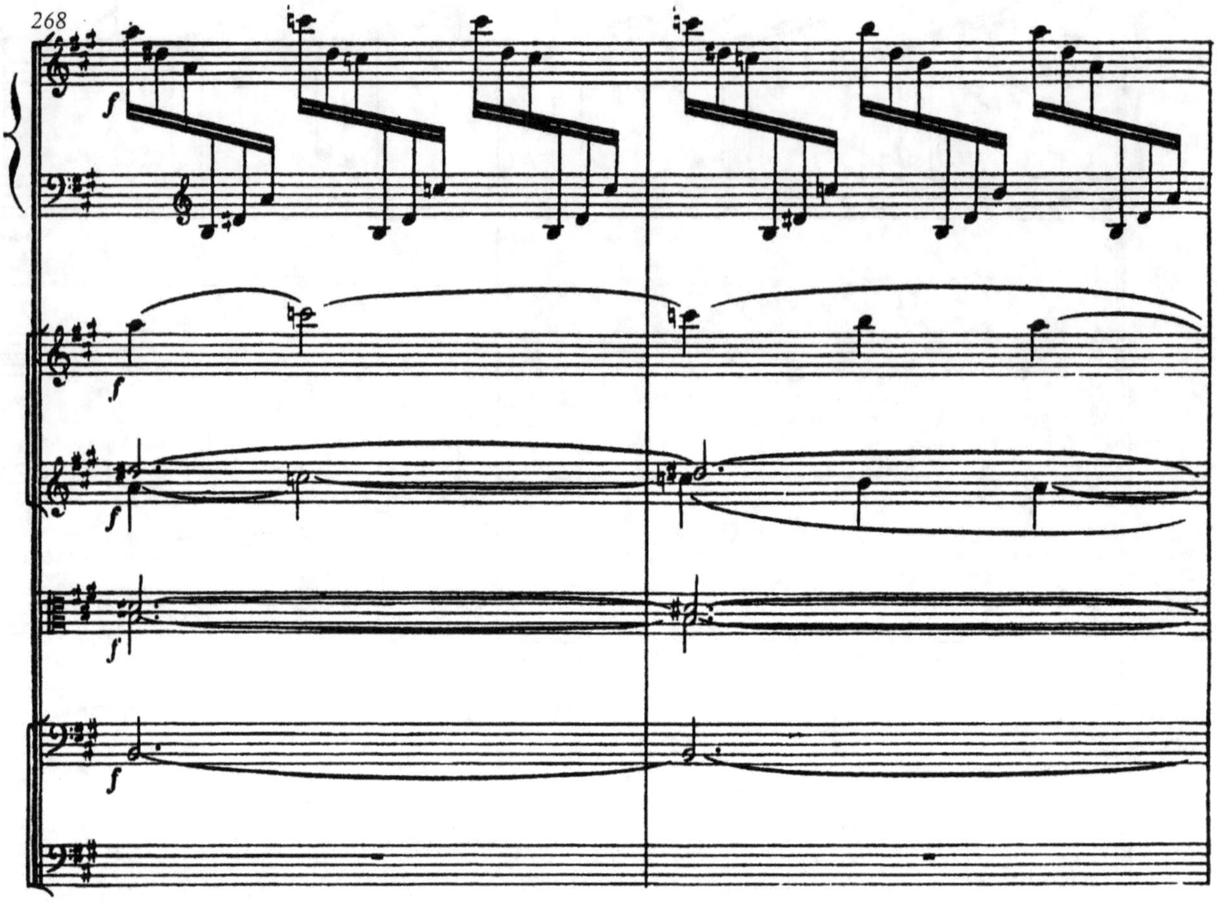
268
f
f
f
f
f

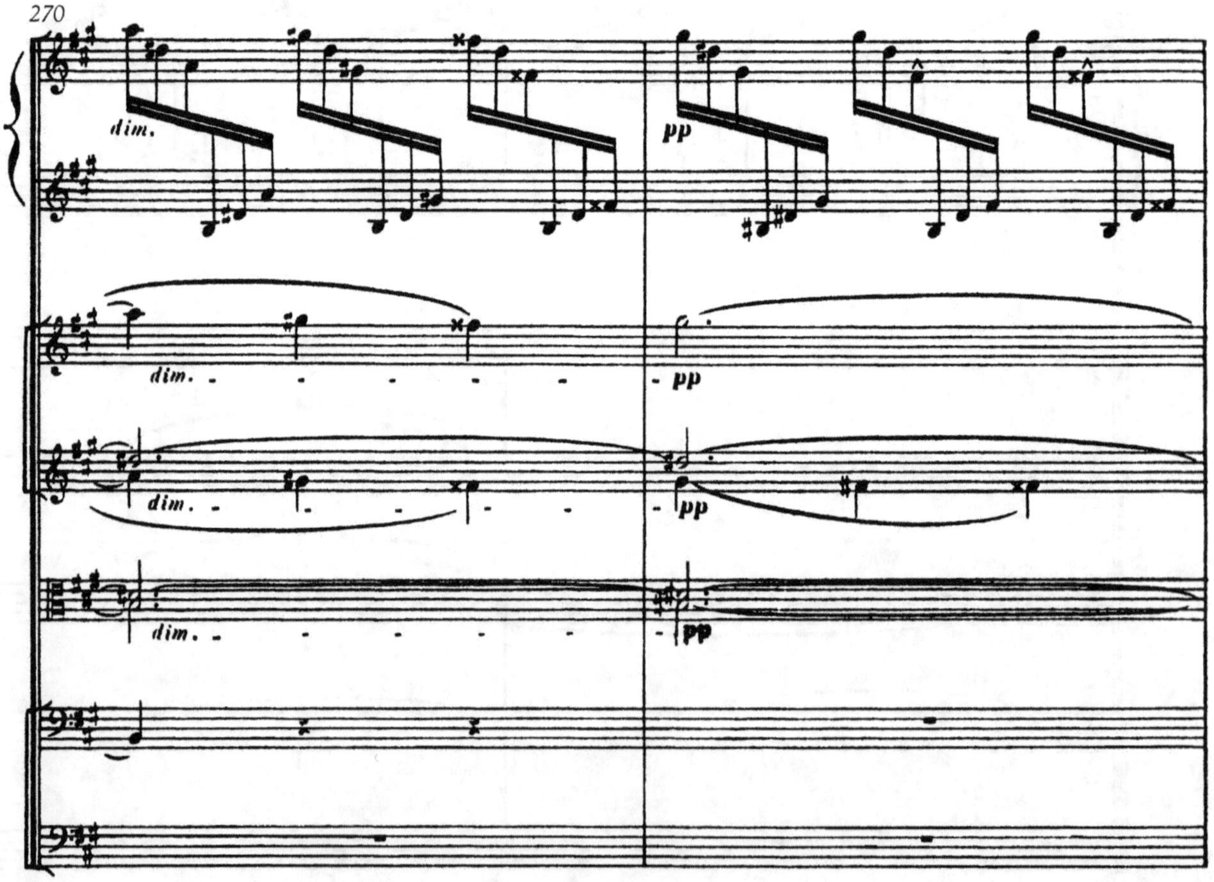
270
dim.
pp
dim.
pp
dim.
pp
dim.
pp

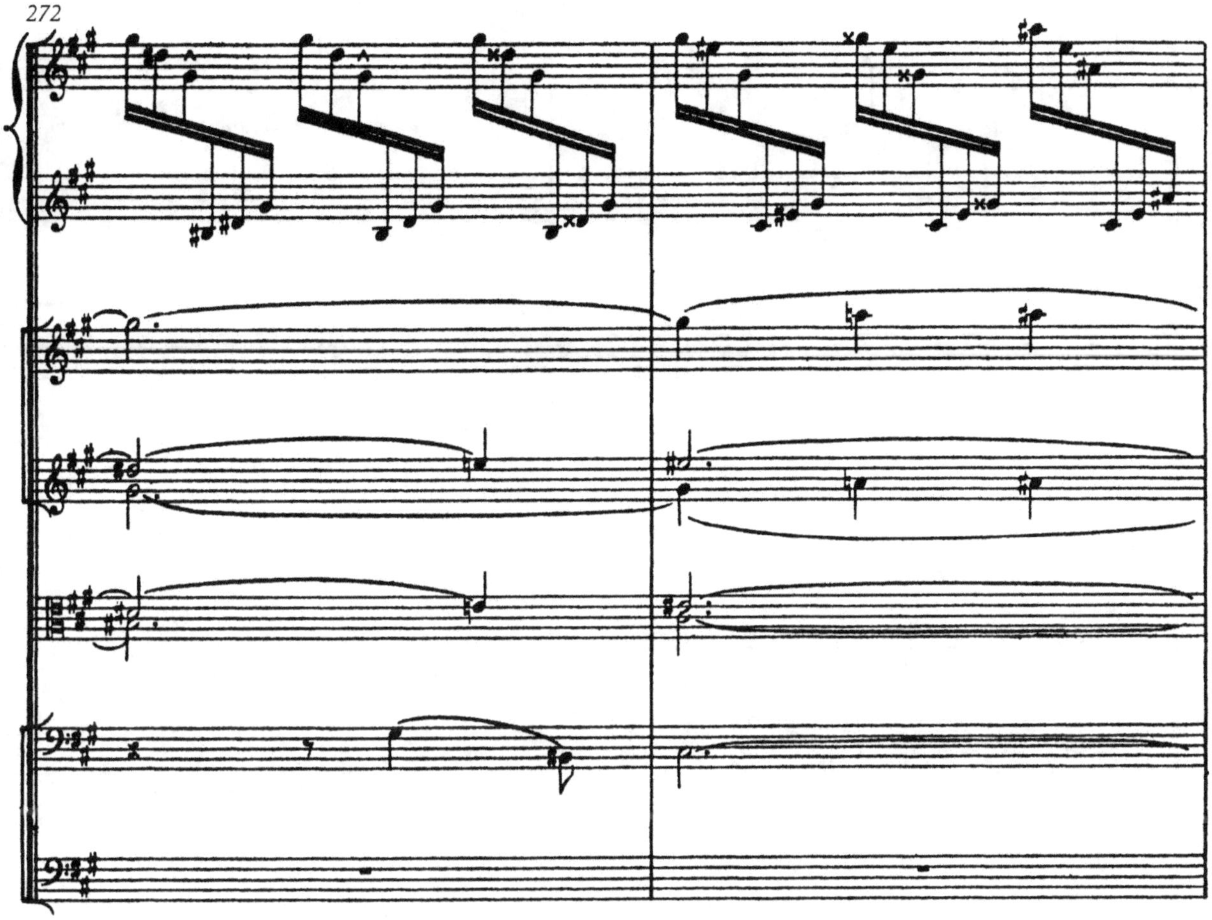
272

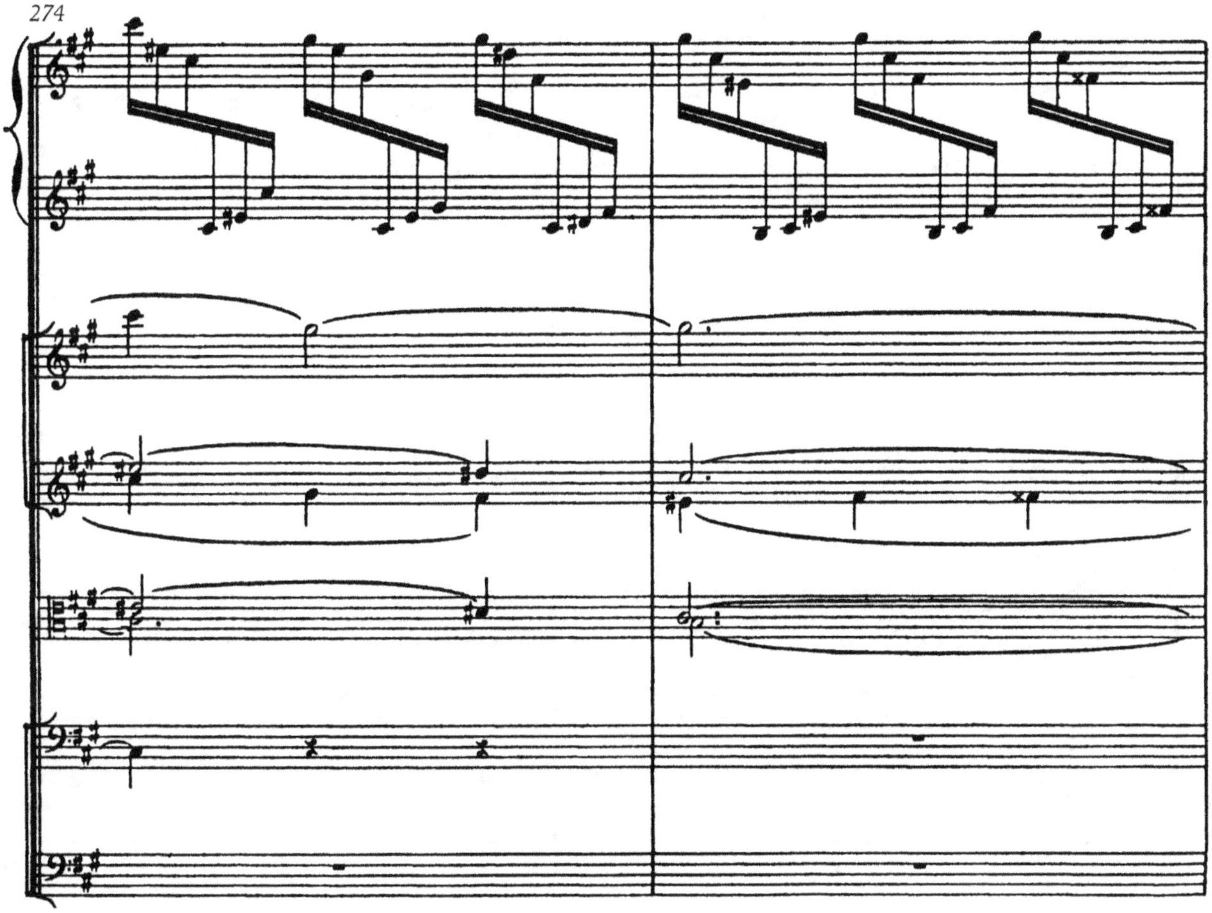
274

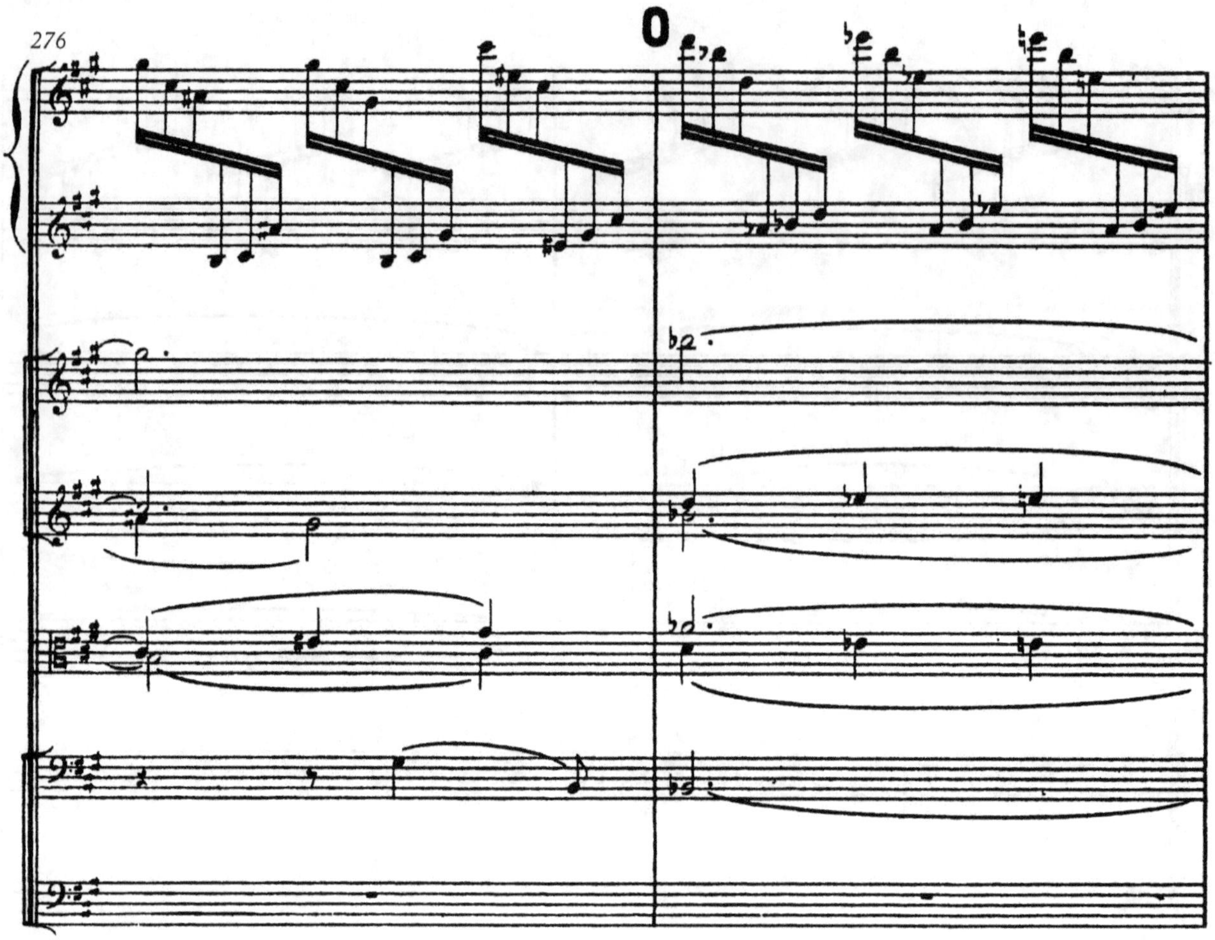
276
O

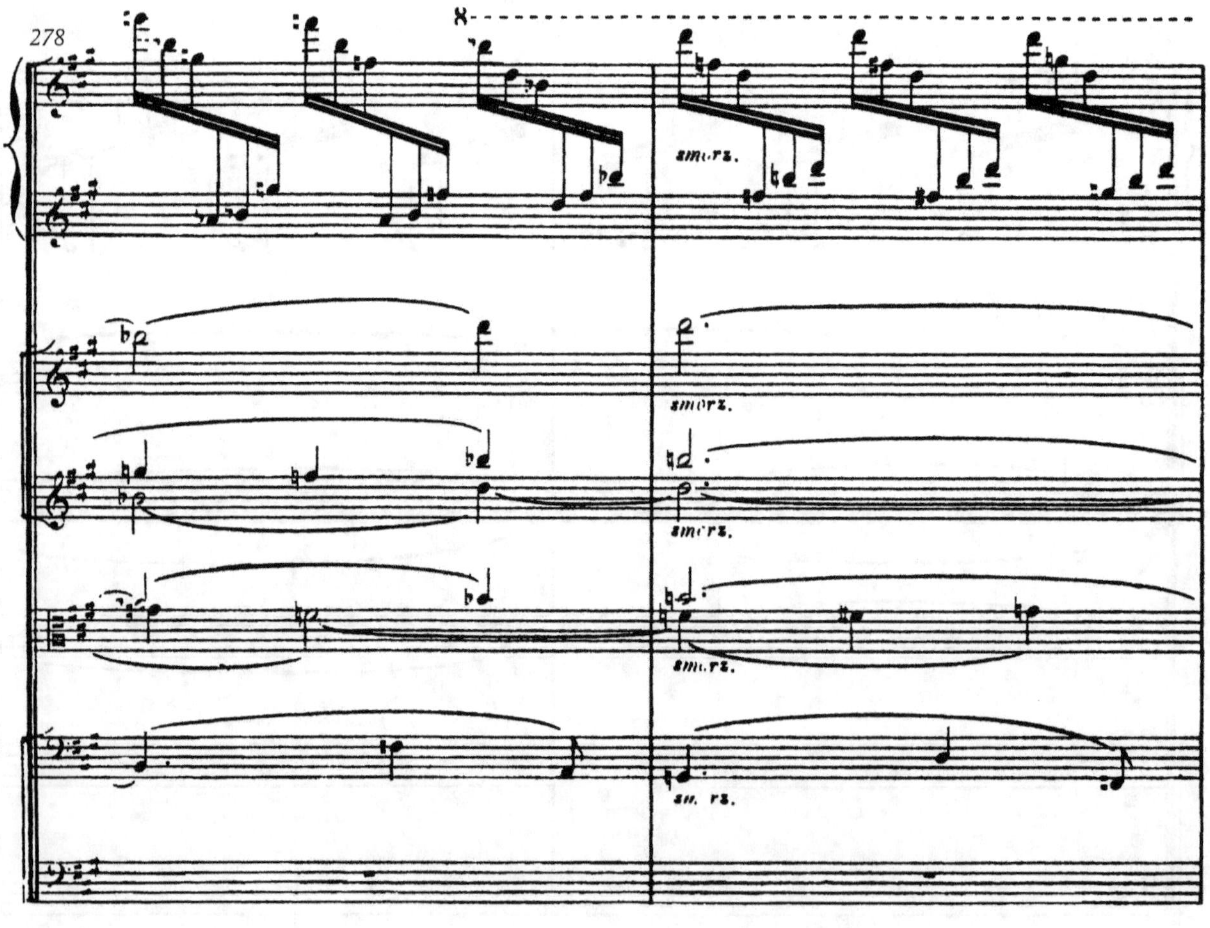
278
8
smorz.
smorz.
smorz.
smorz.
smorz.

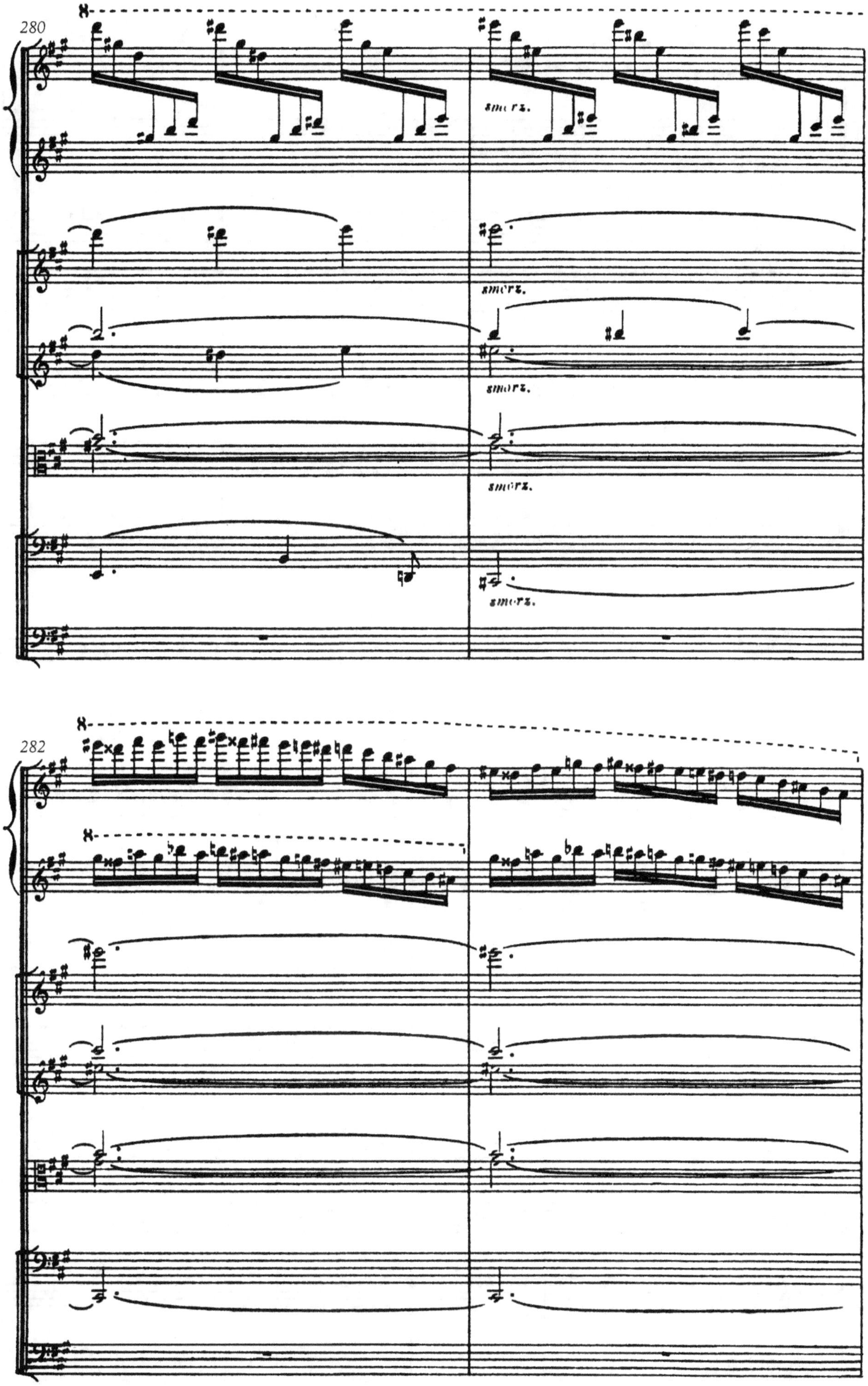
280
smorz.
smorz.
smorz.
smorz.
smorz.
282

All° non troppo.
284
Otez la Sourdine.
Otez la Sourdine.
Otez la Sourdine.
Otez la Sourdine.
All° non troppo.
288
Hauth.
pp
Clar.
pp
B°ns
pp
1.r et 2e Cors.
à 2
pp
288
Piano.
Vns
Altos.
Vclles et C. B.
pp

294 Fl.
Hauth.
Clar.
Bns
Cors.
Tromp.
Timb.
pp
294
Piano.
pizz.
pp
Vns
Div. pizz.
pp
Altos.
Unis.
pp
Velles et C. B.

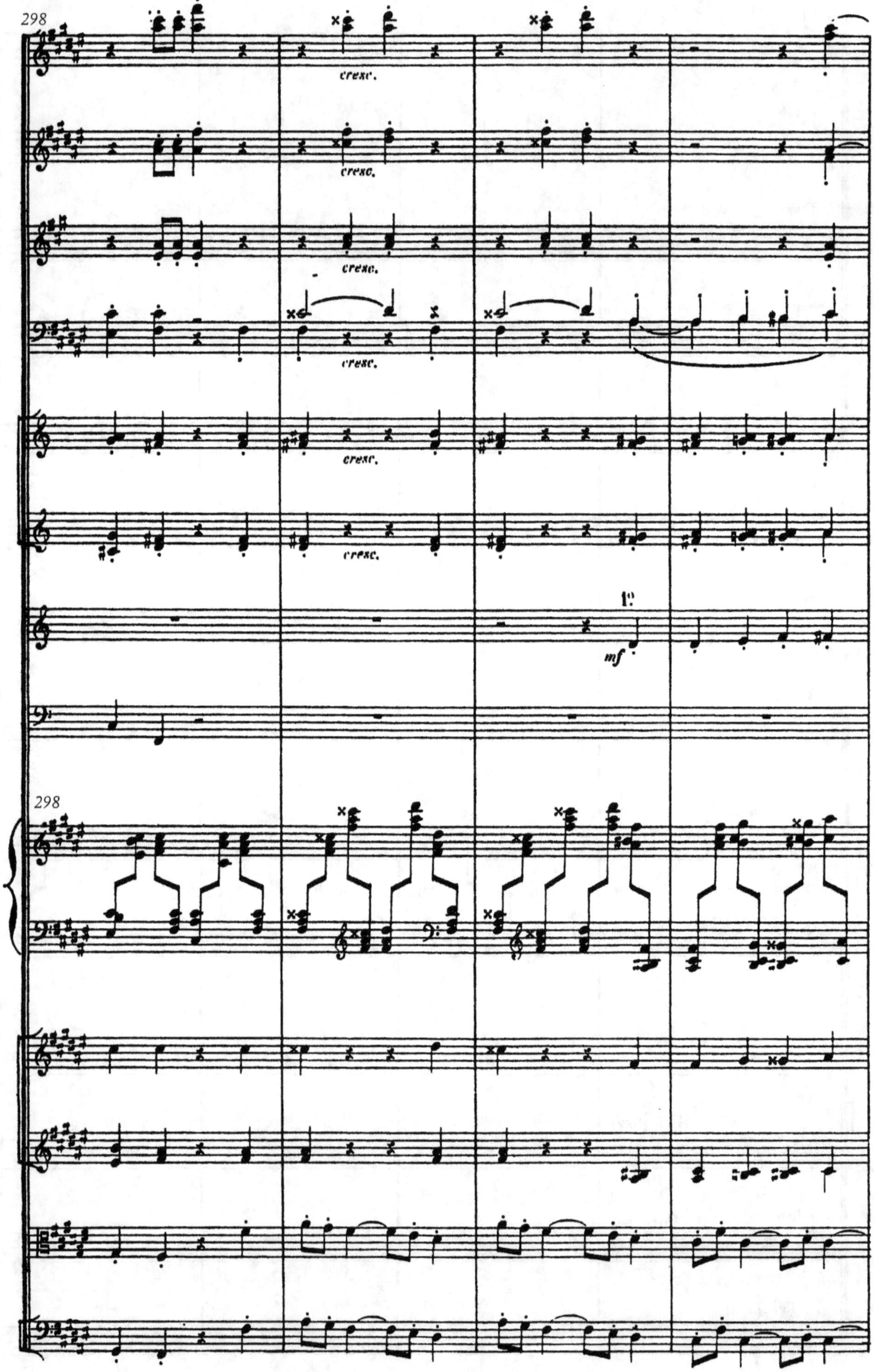
298
cresc.
cresc.
cresc.
cresc.
cresc.
cresc.
1º
mf
298

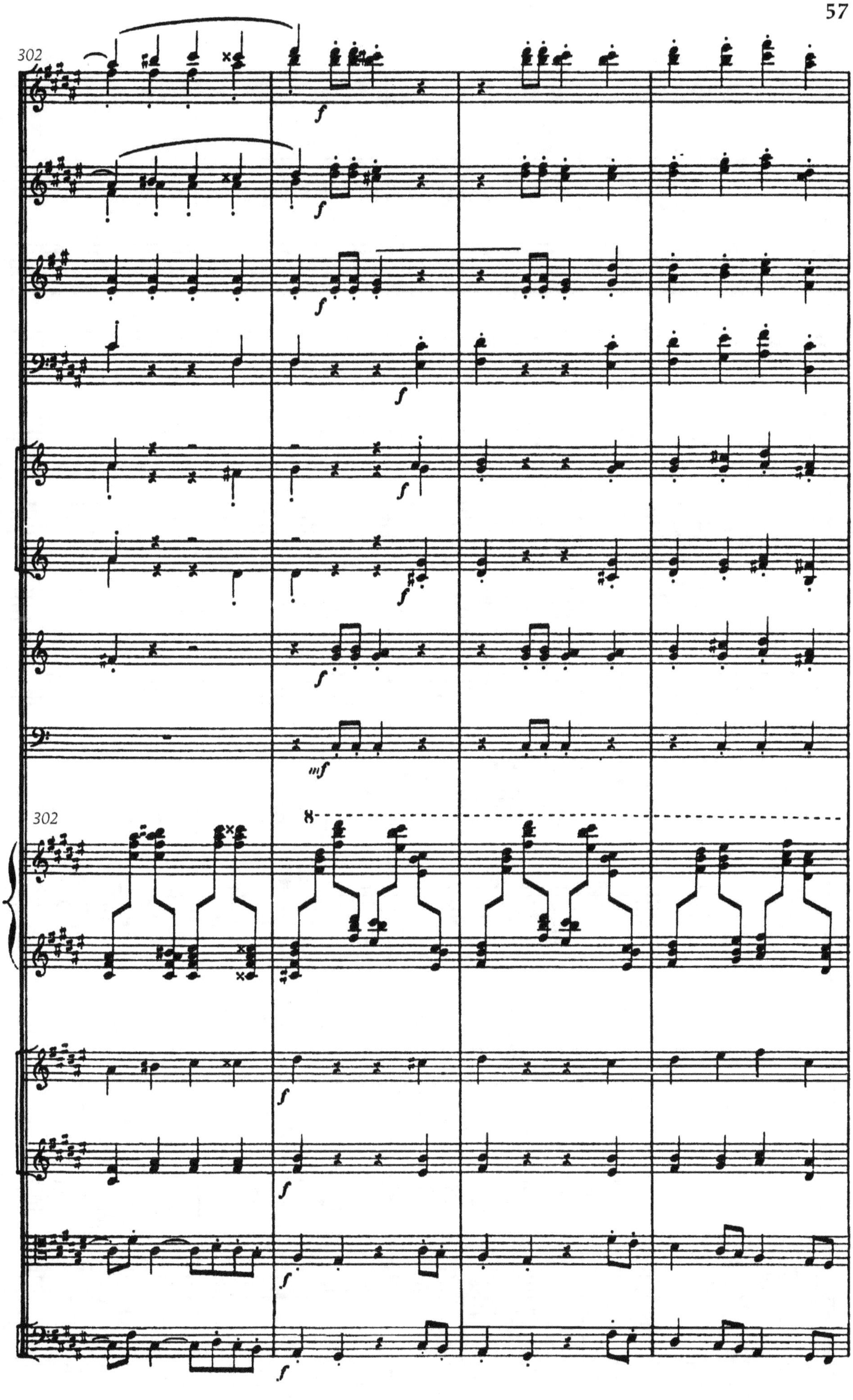
302
f
mf
302
8

P
306
306
8
f con fuoco.
arco.
f
pizz.
arco.
arco.
f
pizz.
arco.
pizz.
arco.
f
Velles
pizz.
arco.
f
C. B.

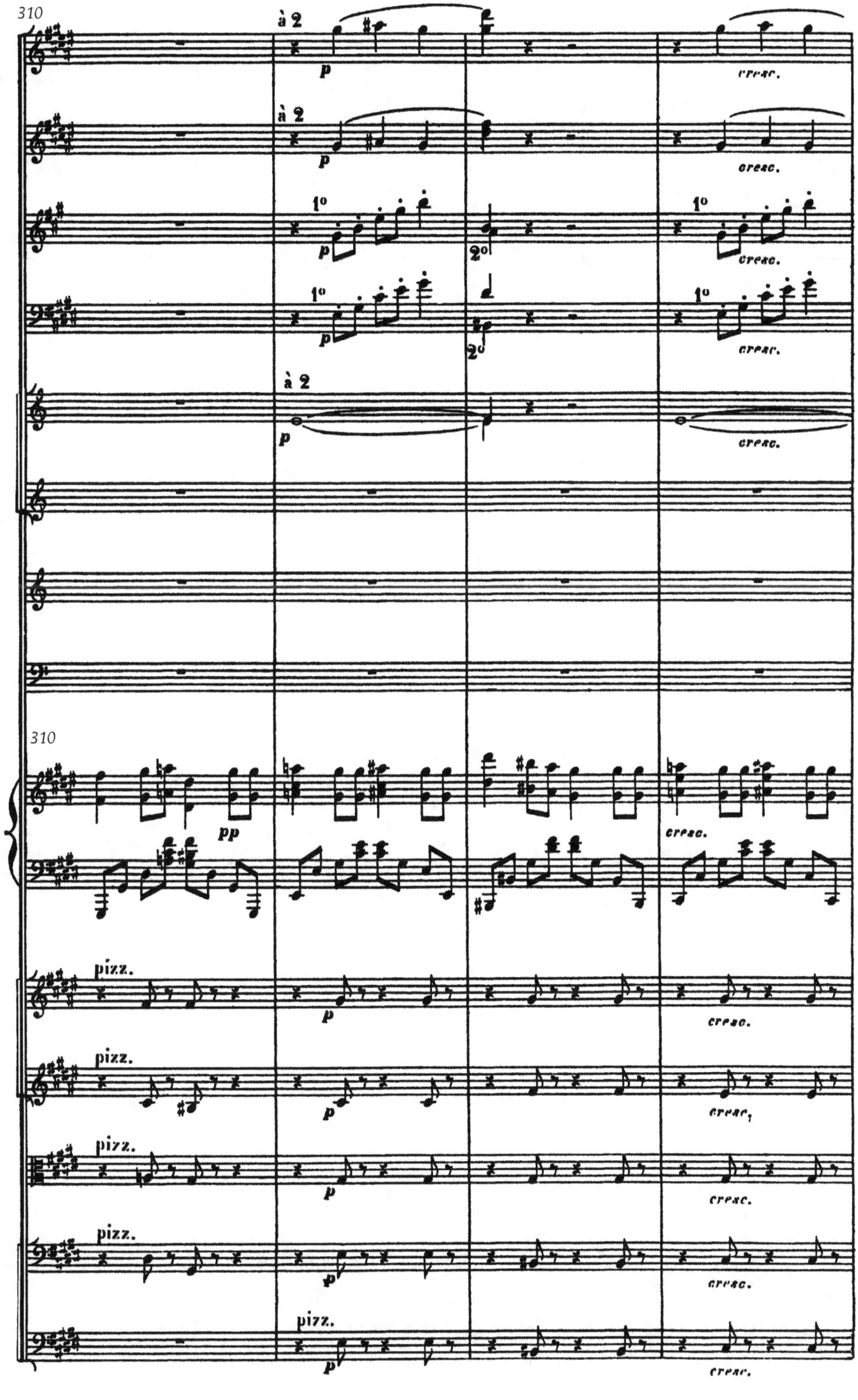
310
à 2
p
cresc.
1o
2o
pp
pizz.

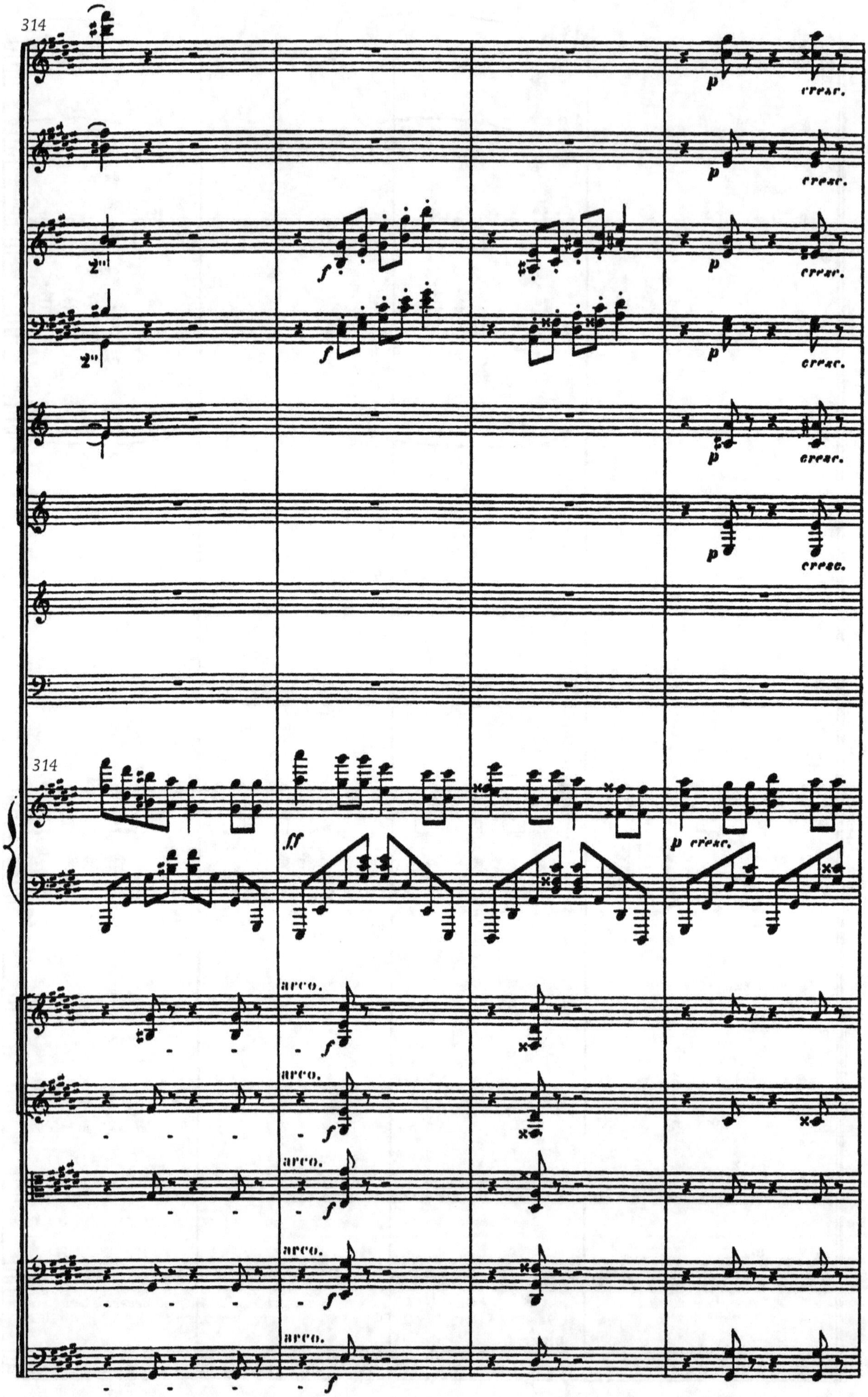
314
p
cresc.
f
ff
p cresc.
arco.

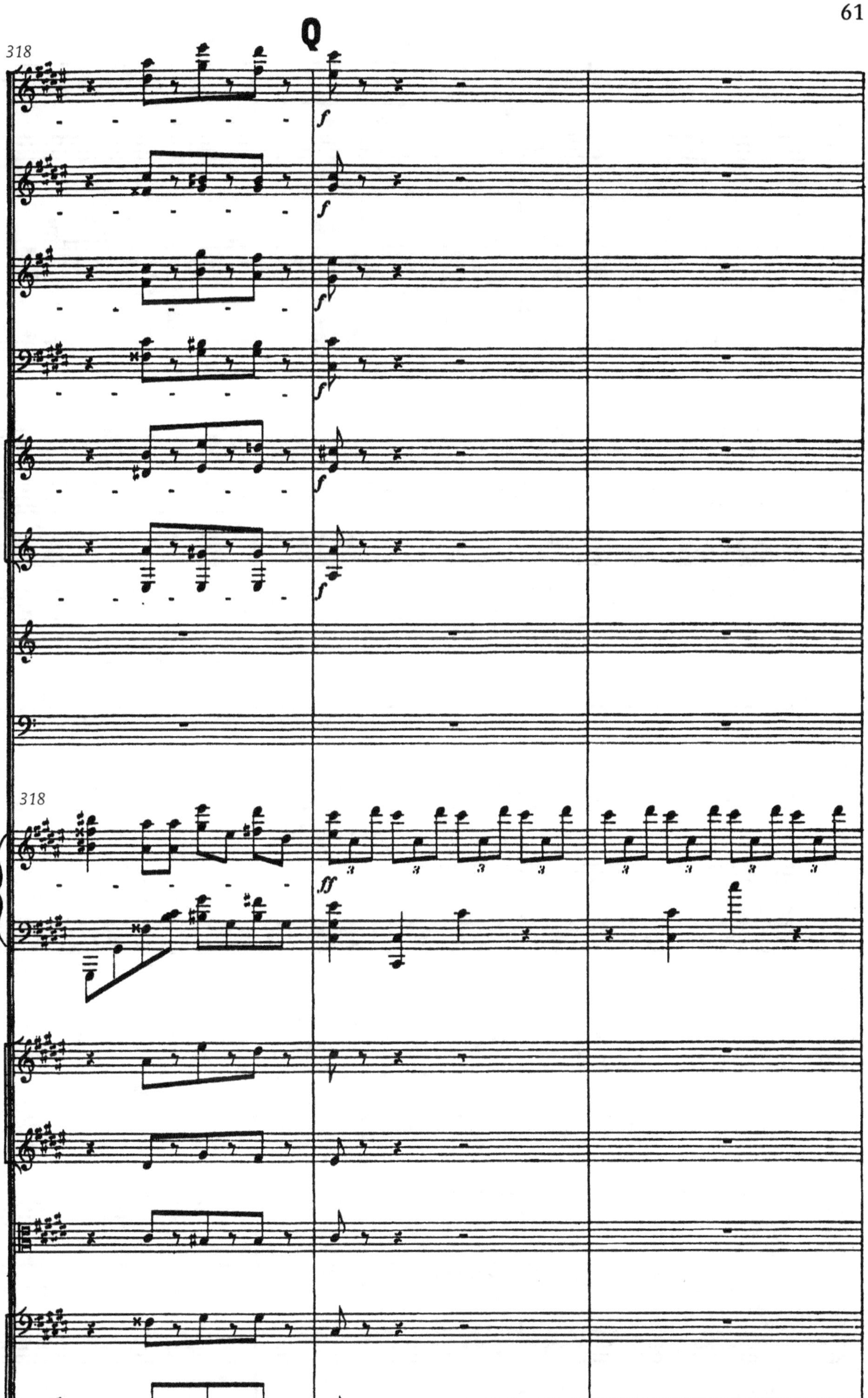
Q
318
318
f
ff

321
Clar.
1rs et 2es Cors.
p
p
321
dim.
p
Piano.
Vons
Altos.
Velles et C.B.
324
Fl.
1º
mf
f
Hautb.
1º
mf
f
Clar.
f
Cors 1º et 2º
f
324
f
Piano.
pizz.
mf
Vons
pizz.
mf
Altos.
pizz.
mf
Velles
pizz.
mf
C.B.

327
dim.
dim.
dim.
dim.
p
327
8
dim.
p
p
p
p
p
330
Clar.
cresc.
p
Cors 1° et 2°
cresc.
p
330
p
cresc.
Piano.
molto cresc.
Vns
molto cresc.
molto cresc.
molto cresc.

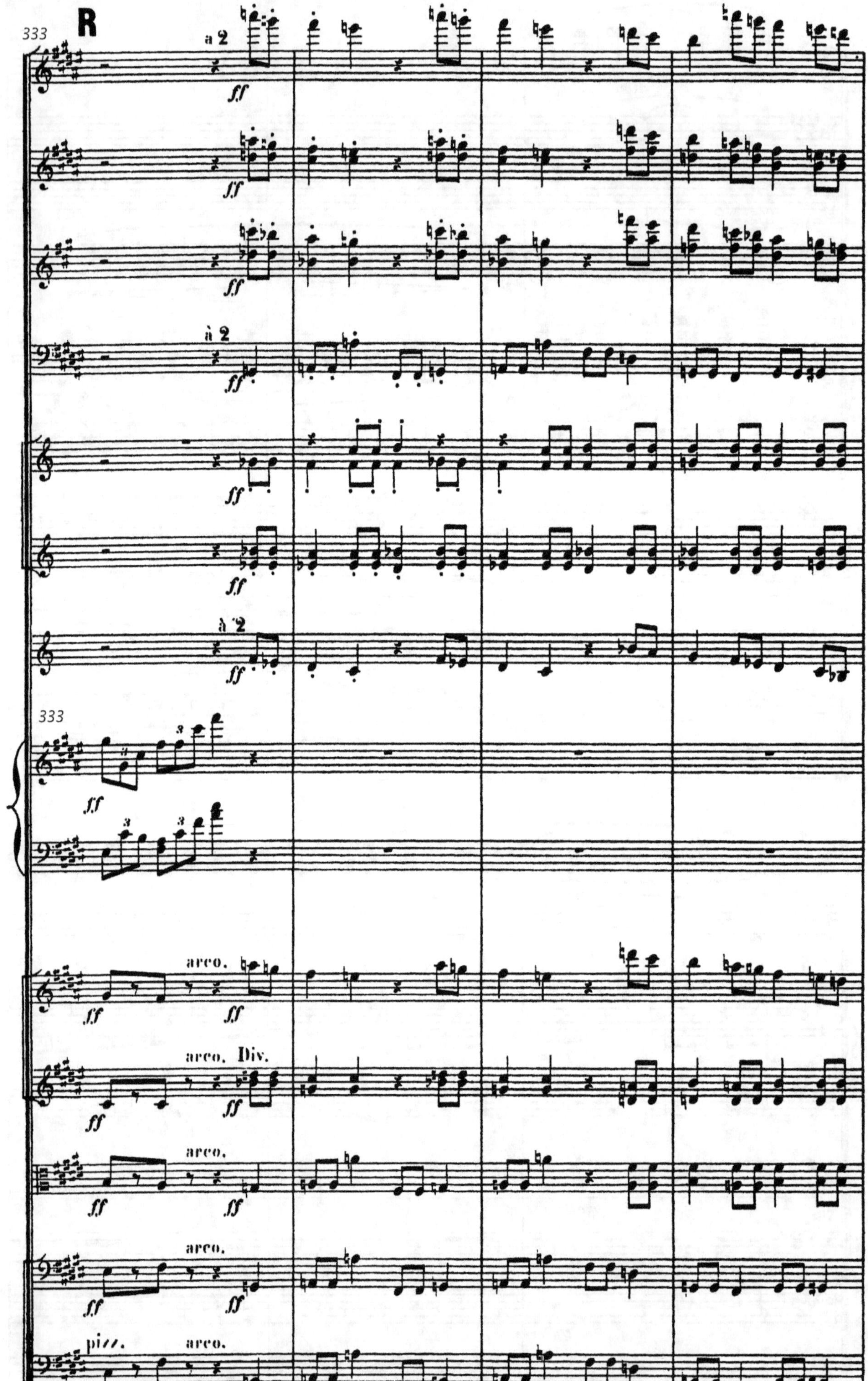
333
R
a 2
ff
à 2
333
arco.
arco. Div.
pizz.

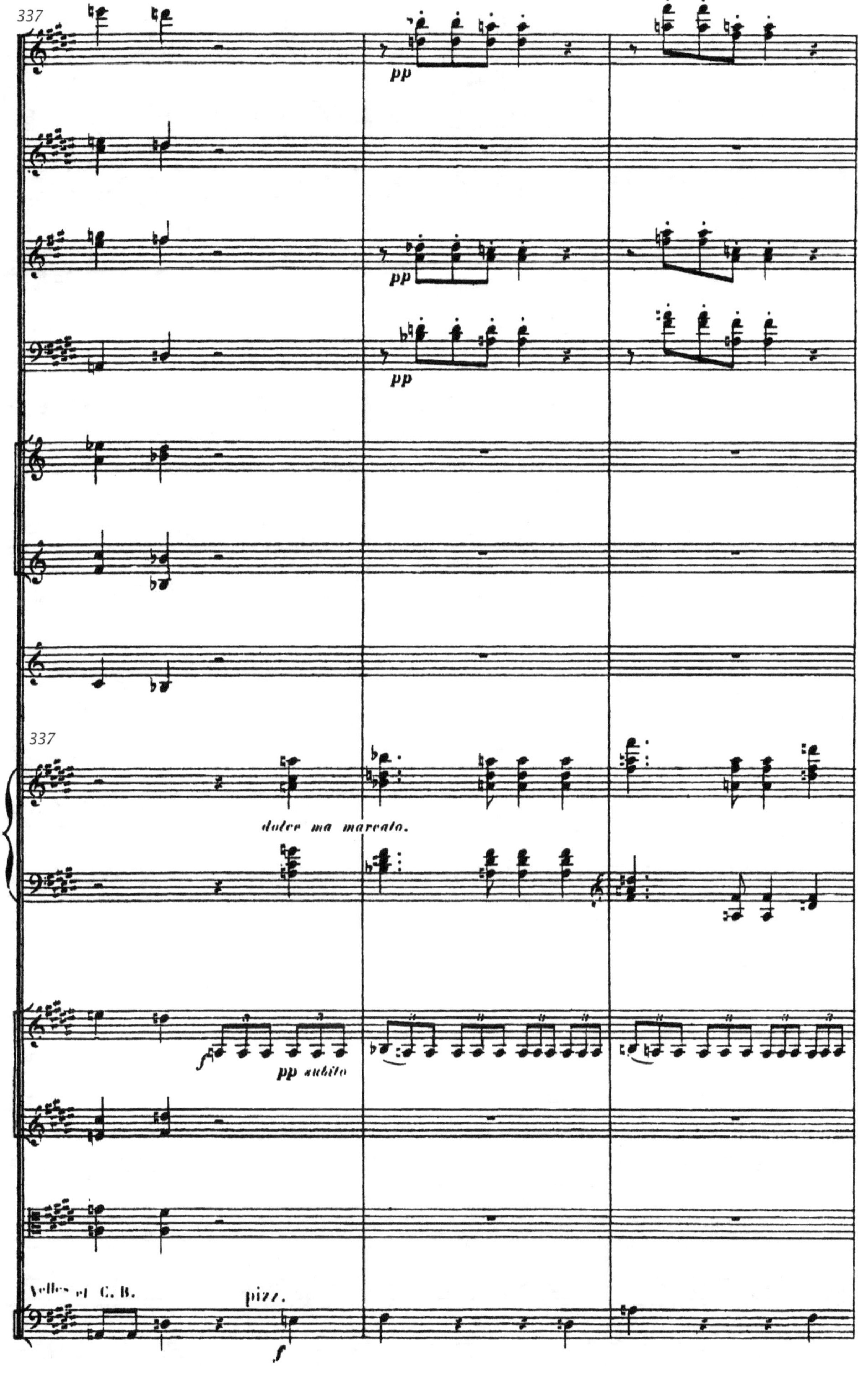
337
pp
pp
pp
337
dolce ma marcato.
pp subito
Velles et C. B.
pizz.
f

340
Clar.
poco cresc.
Piano.
cresc.
Vns
Altos.
Velles et C.B.
344
Fl.
S
1º
p
1r et 2e Cors.
à 2
pp
Div.
pizz. p
Velles
Div. pizz.
C.B.
pizz.

347
Clar.
Bns
1er et 2e Cors.
347
Piano.
pizz.
Vns
Altos.
p
Velles
Unis.
C.B.
350
Fl.
pp
Clar.
pp
Bns
pp
350
Piano.
Vns
Altos.
Velles et C.B.

353
Hauth.
cresc.
f
Clar.
cresc.
à 2.
p
Bns
à 2.
1er et 2e Cors.
Piano.
arco.
Vlns
Altos
Velles et C. B.
357
Div.
Velles
C.B.

363
à 2.
Fl.
f
cresc.
ff
Hautb.
Clar.
Bns
Cors.
Tromp.
1º
357
Piano.
dolce
Vns
Altos.
Unis.
Vlles
C.B.

Un pochettino rit°.
368
Piano.
Un pochettino rit°.
Altos.
Velles et C.B.
Un pochettino rit°.
371
374
molto dolce.

377
380
T
Tempo 1º.
384
Fl.
1º.
p
384
Piano.
f
dim.
Tempo 1º.
Vns
Altos.
Vlles et C.B.
Tempo 1º.

386 Fl.
Clar.
pp
Bns
pp
386
Piano. pp
Vns
Altos.
Vlles et C.B.
389 Fl.
Hautb.
1o
mf
Clar.
Bns
1o
mf
389
Piano.
Vns
Altos.
Div.
p
Vlles
Div.
p
C.B.

392
Fl.
U
mf
Hautb.
mf
Clar.
mf
Bns
mf
Cors.
mf
mf
Tromp.
Timb.
392
Piano.
sempre cresc.
Vns
mf
mf
Altos
Unis.
mf
Vncs
mf
C.B. pizz.
p
arco.
mf

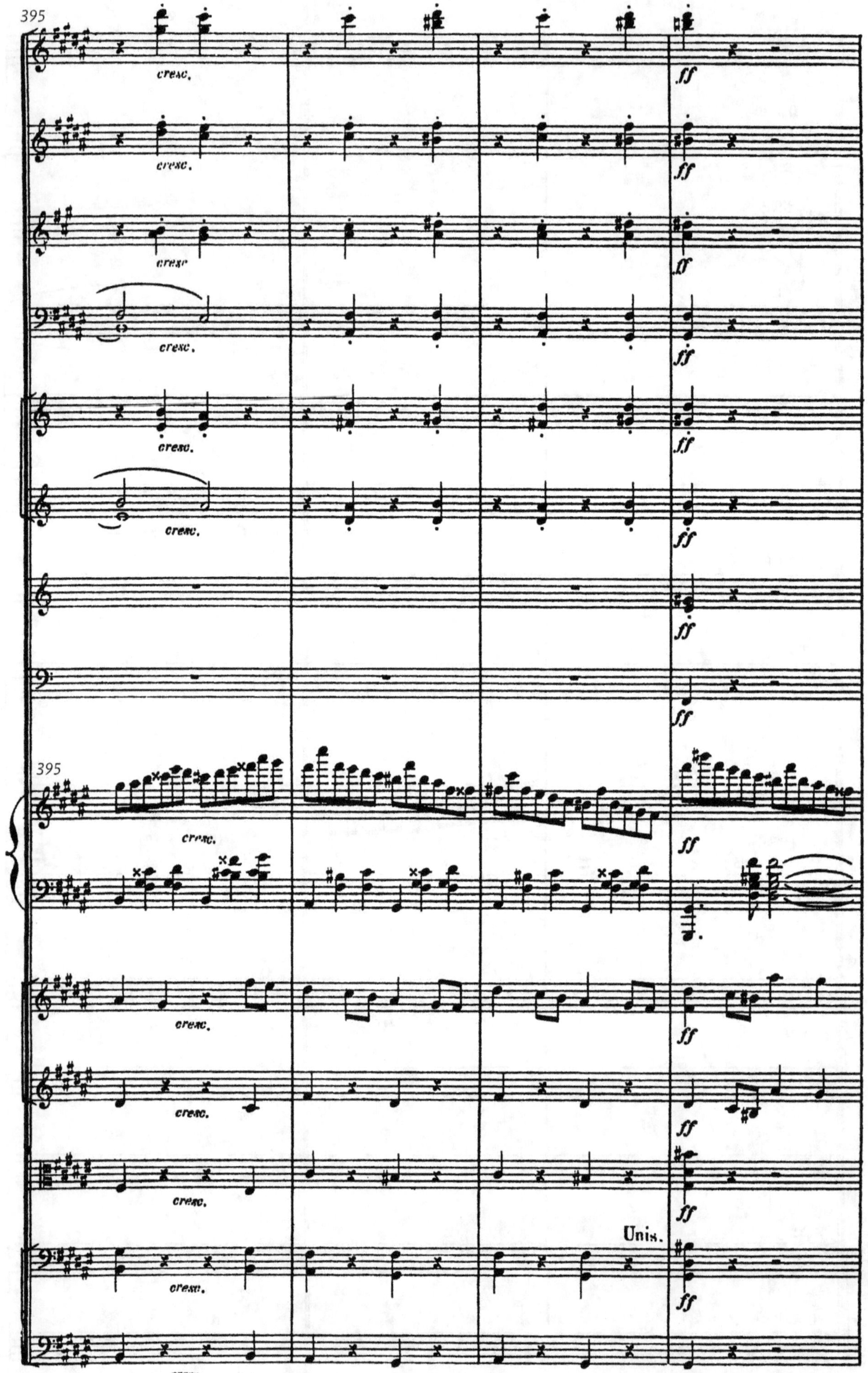
395
cresc.
ff
Unis.

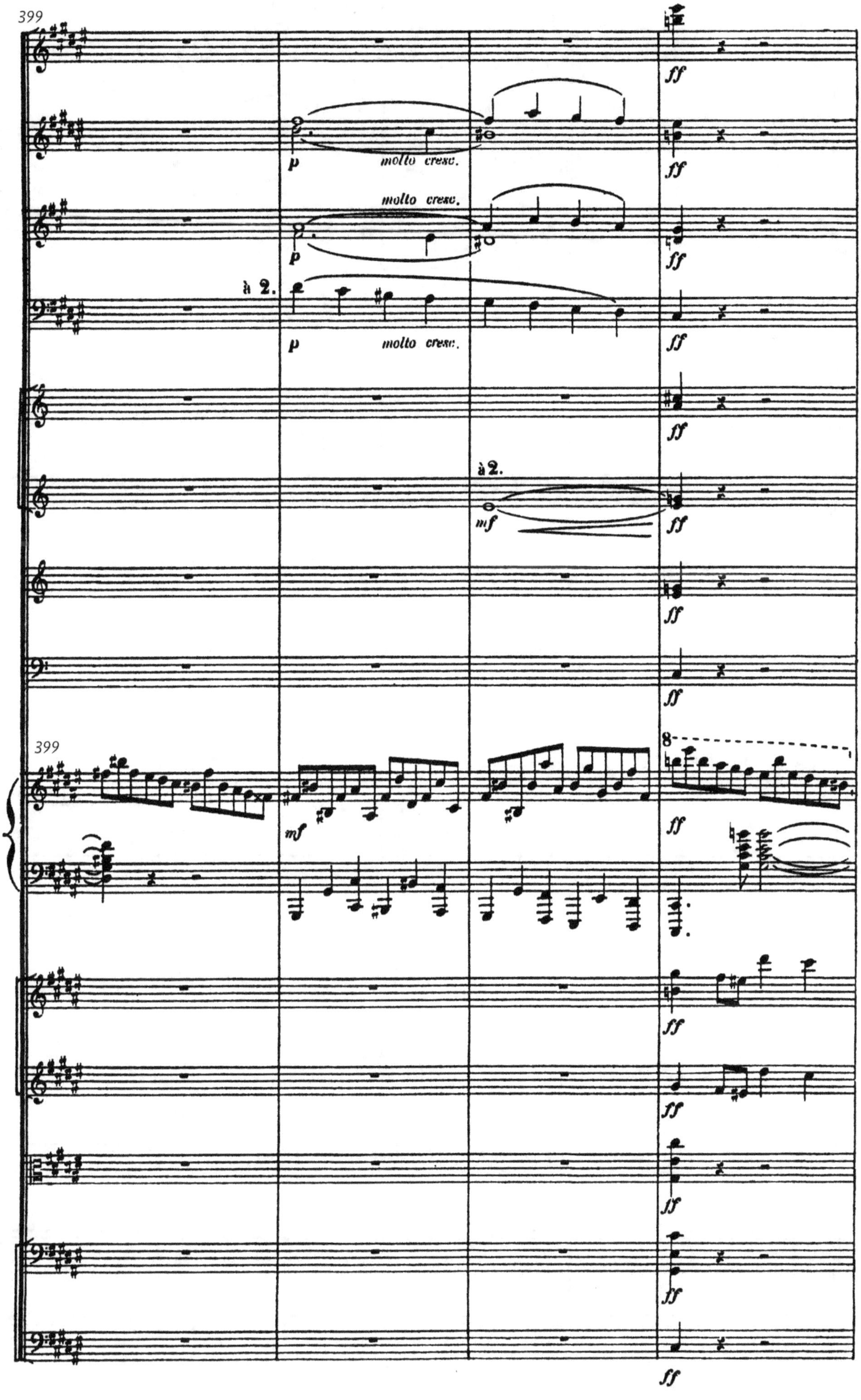
399
molto cresc.
molto cresc.
à 2.
molto cresc.
à 2.
399
8

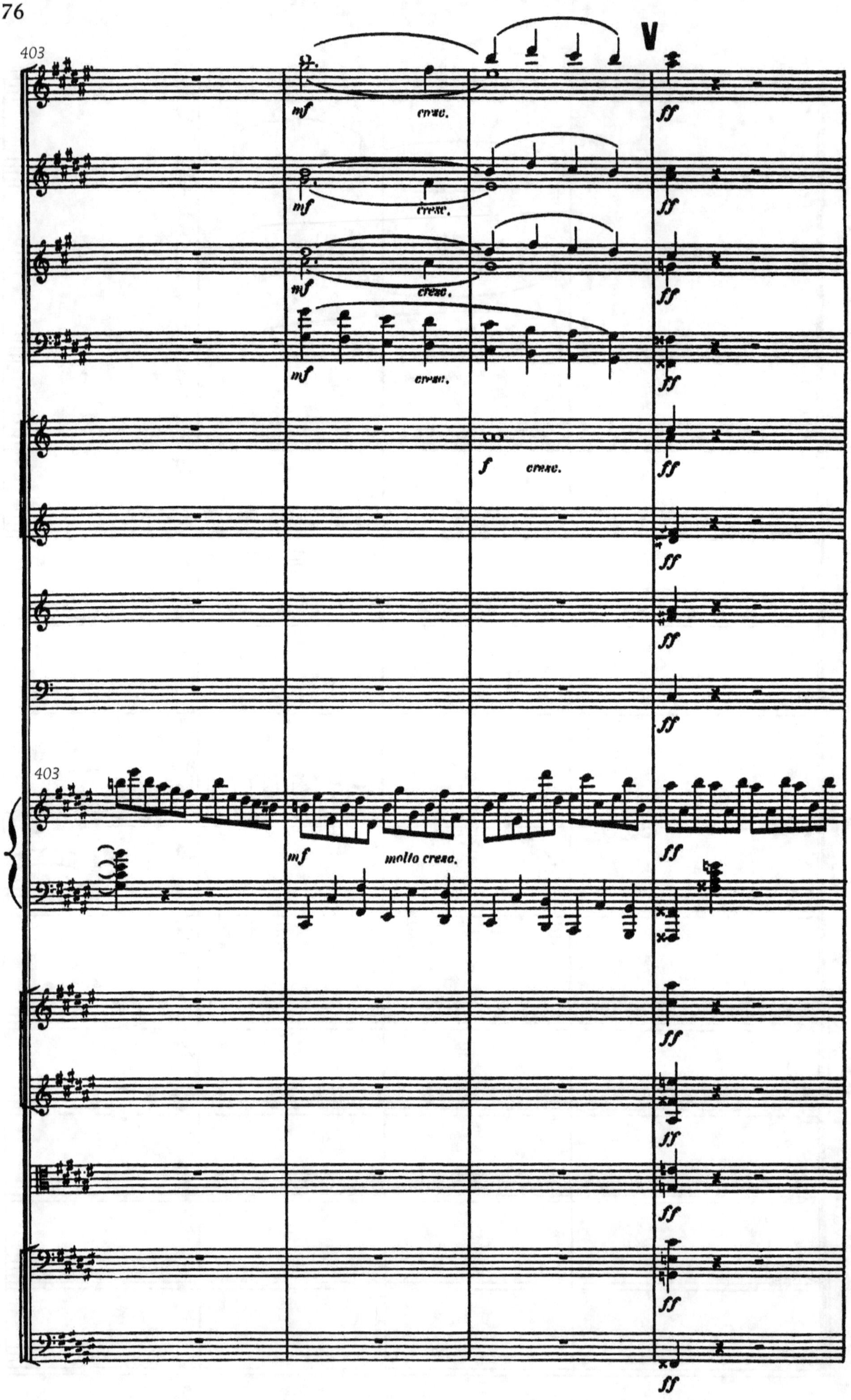
403
mf
cresc.
V
ff
f
molto cresc.

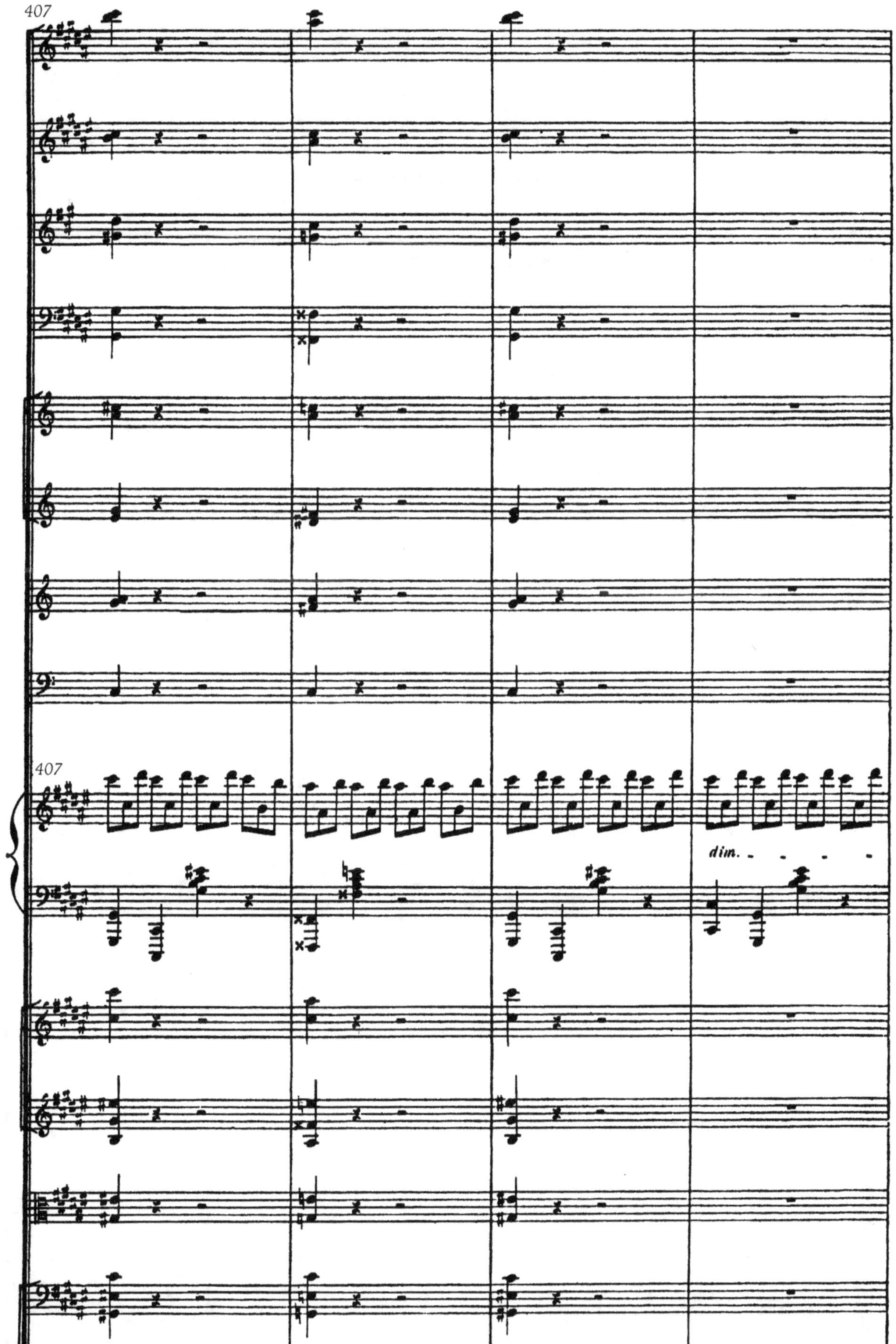
407
407
dim.

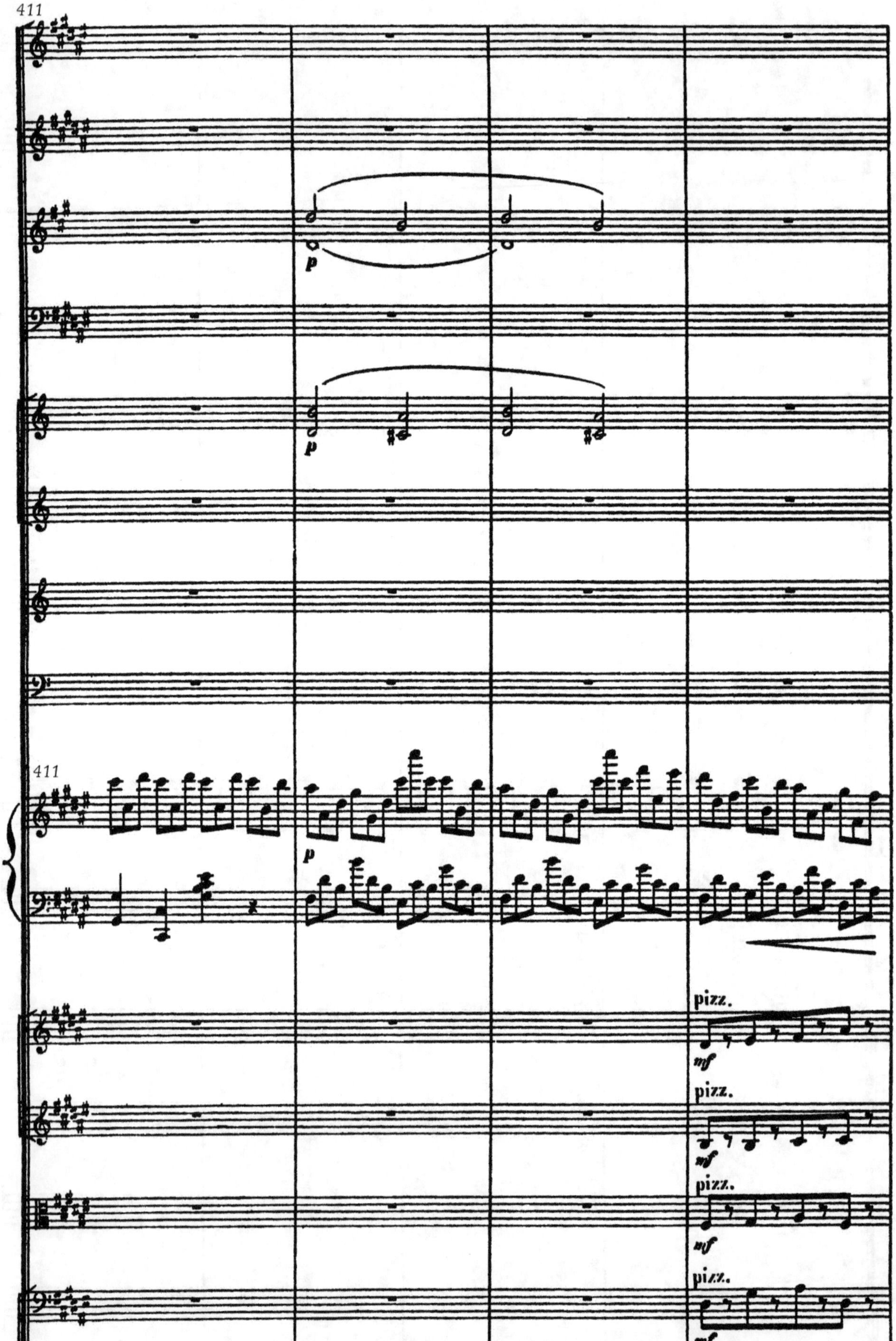
411
p
p
411
p
pizz.
mf
pizz.
mf
pizz.
mf
pizz.
mf

415
1º
mf
cresc.
f
dim.
1º
mf
cresc.
f
dim.
f
dim.
f
dim.
1º
p
415
8
8
f
p
p
p
p
p

419
cresc.
p
cresc.
p
cresc.
2.
p
cresc.
419
p
cresc.
molto.
molto
cresc.
ff
molto
cresc.
ff
molto
cresc.
ff
molto
cresc.
ff

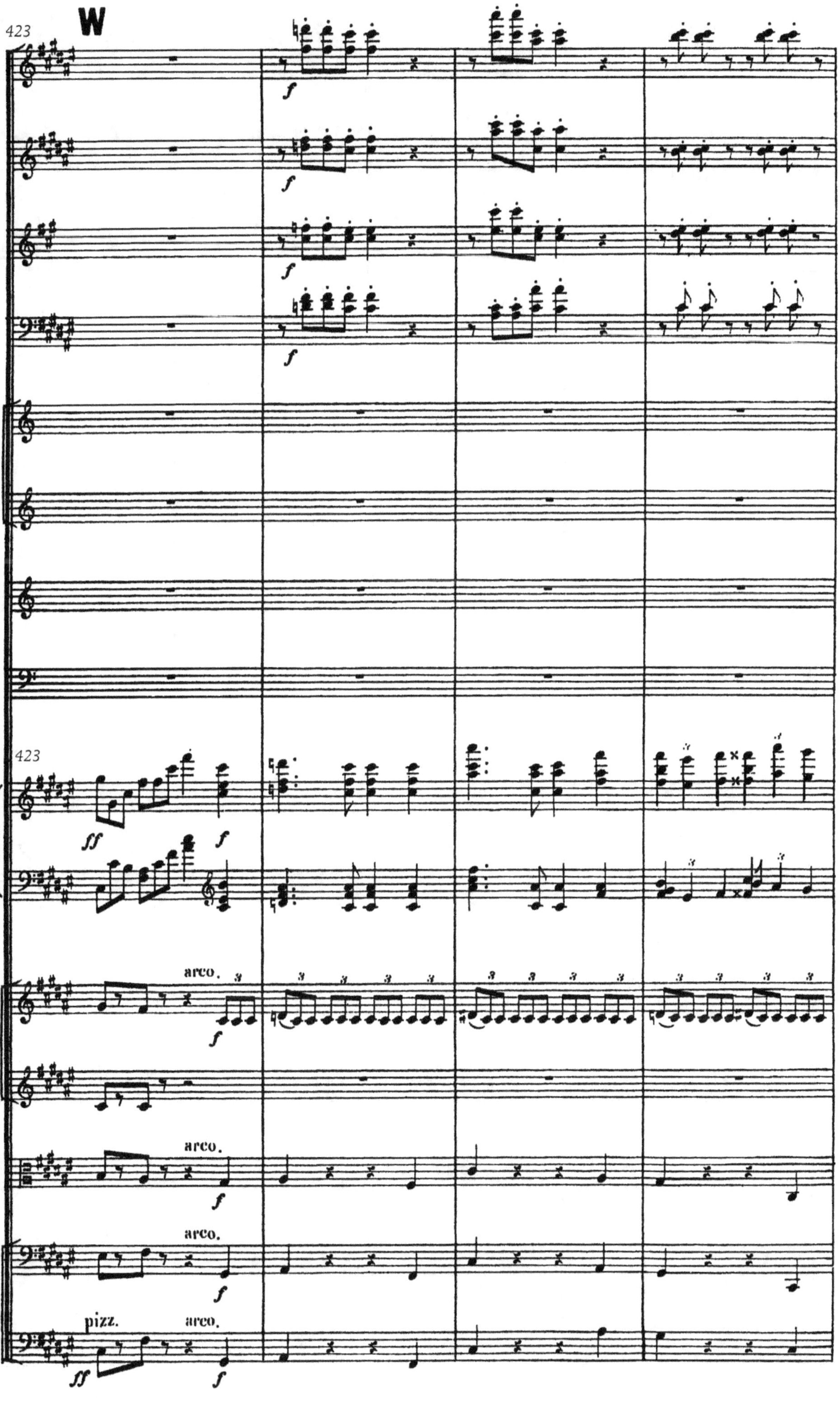
W
423
ff
f
arco.
pizz.

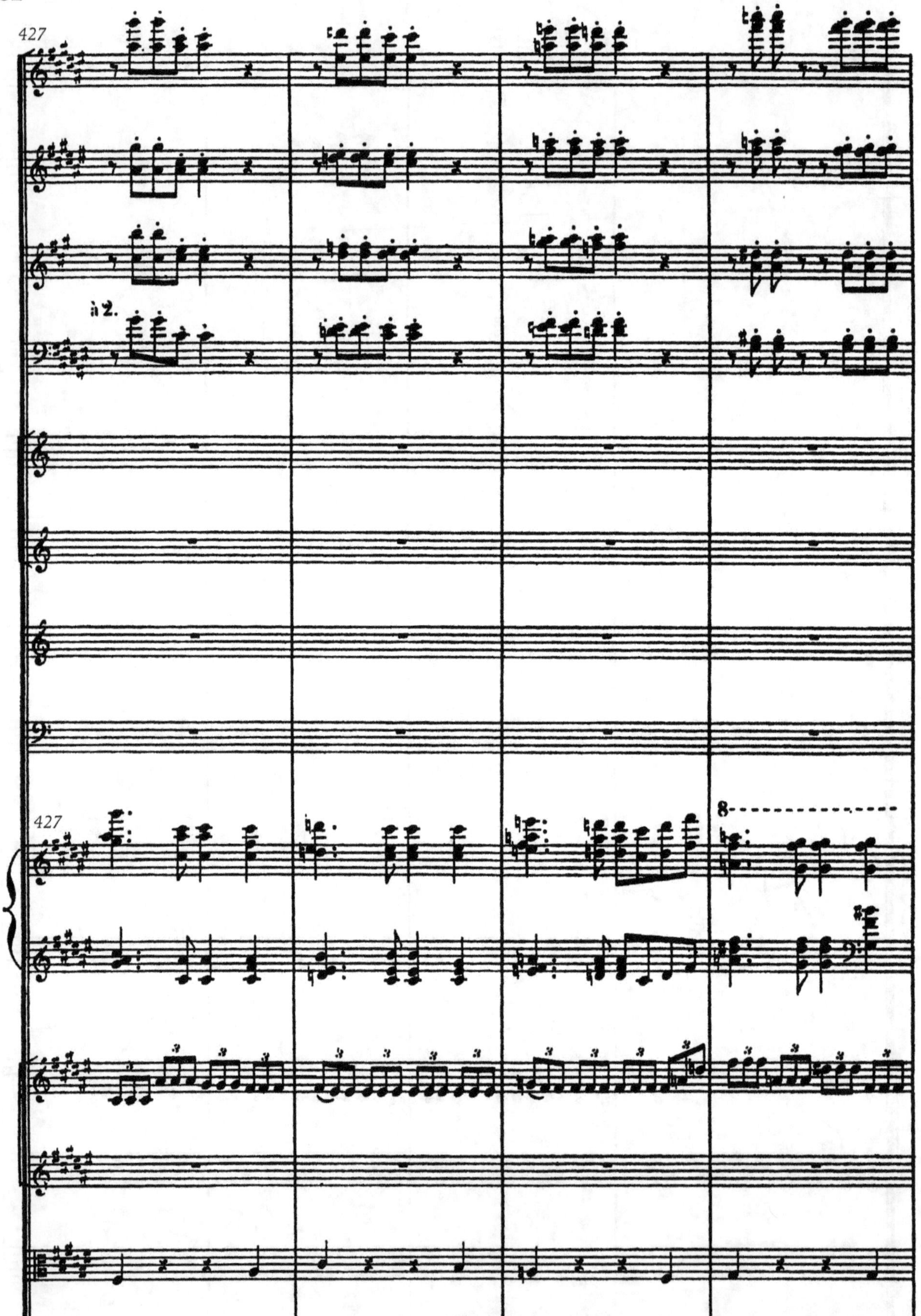
427
à 2.
427
8

436
mf
1º
pp
1º
mf
pp
à 2.
mf
pp
436
8
mf
pp
sempre pizz.
mf
pp
Div. pizz.
mf
pp
mf
pp

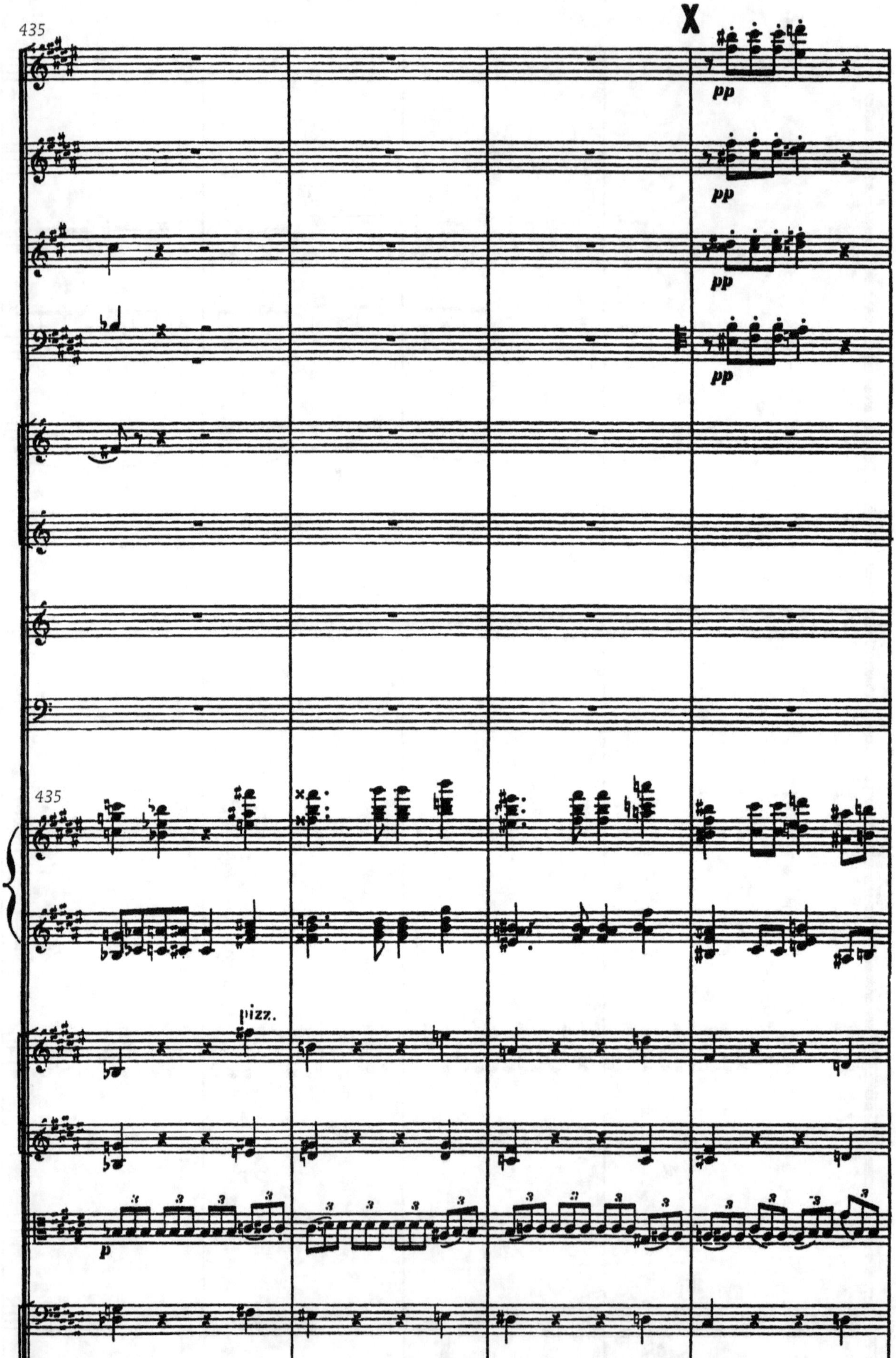
435
X
pp
pp
pp
pp
435
pizz.
p

439
cresc. molto.
cresc. molto.
cresc. molto.
cresc. molto.
ff
ff
ff
ff
mf
cresc.
ff
ff
mf
cresc.
ff
ff
439
8
ff
arco.
cresc. molto.
ff
arco.
cresc. molto.
ff
3
cresc. molto.
ff
arco.
cresc. molto.
ff
arco.
cresc. molto.
ff

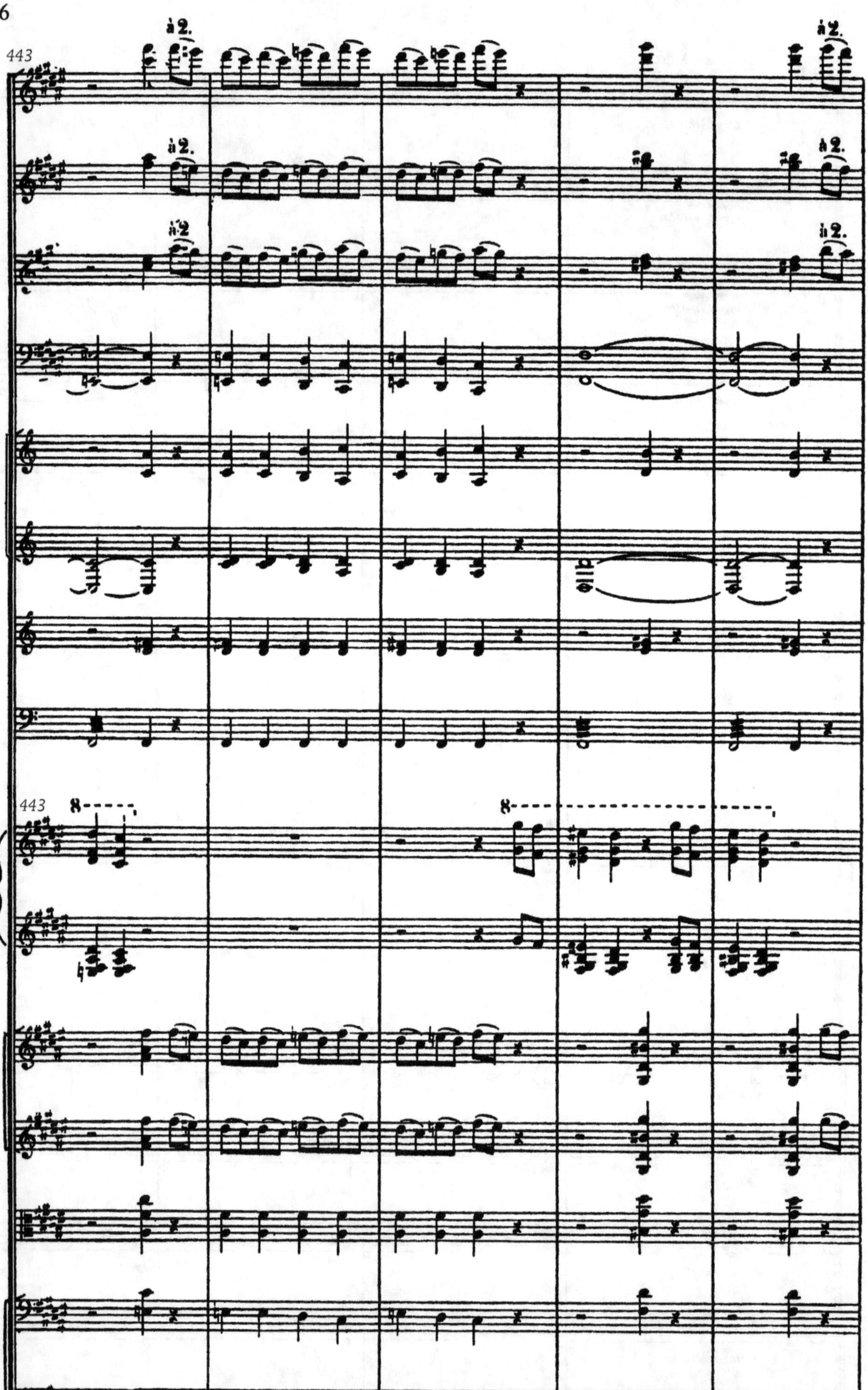
443
à 2.
à 2.
à 2.
à 2.
à 2.
à 2.
443
8

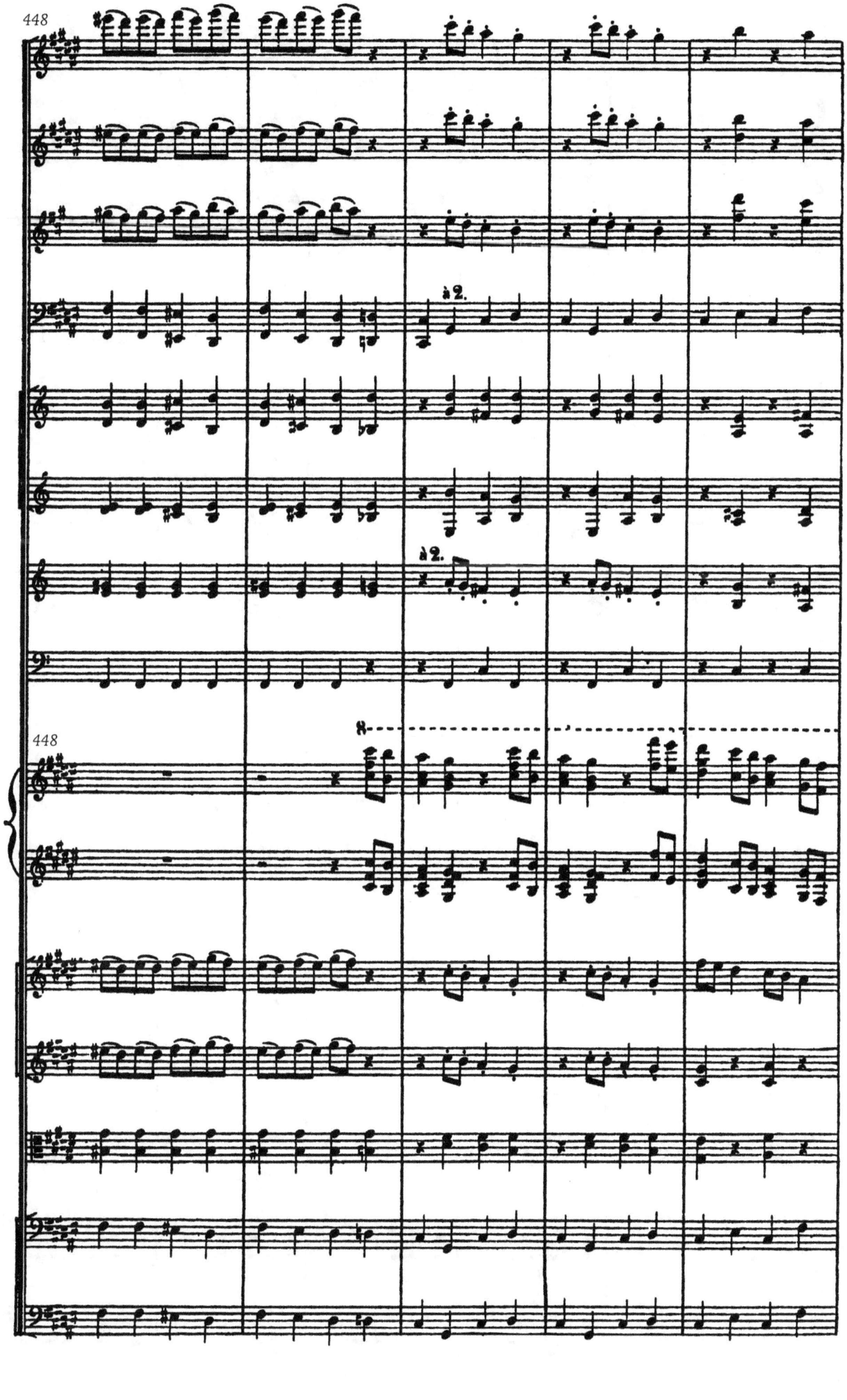
448
à 2.
à 2.
448
8

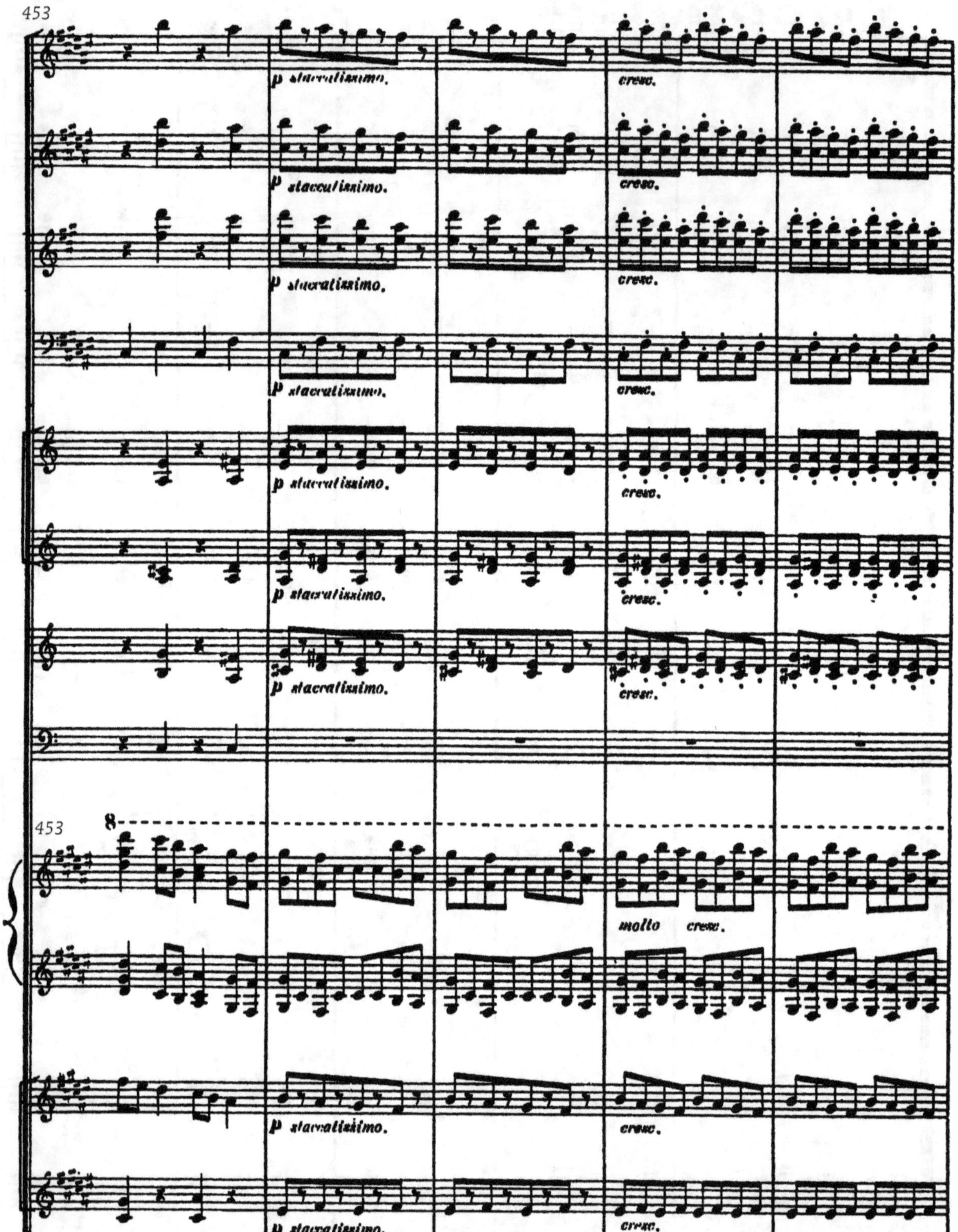
453
p staccatissimo.
cresc.
8
molto cresc.

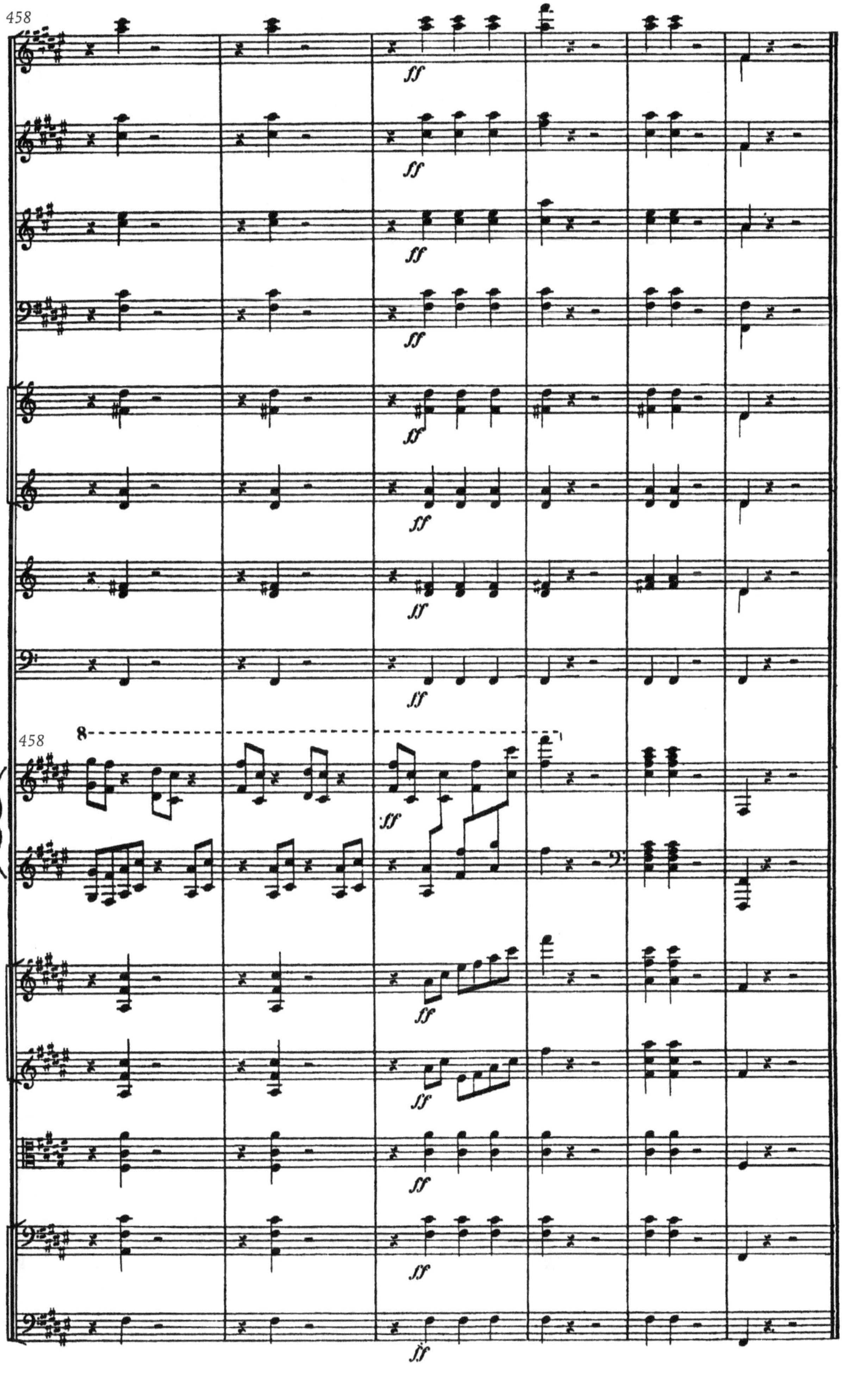
458
ff
458
8
ff